A NATURALIST'S GUIDE
TO THE VIRGINIA COAST

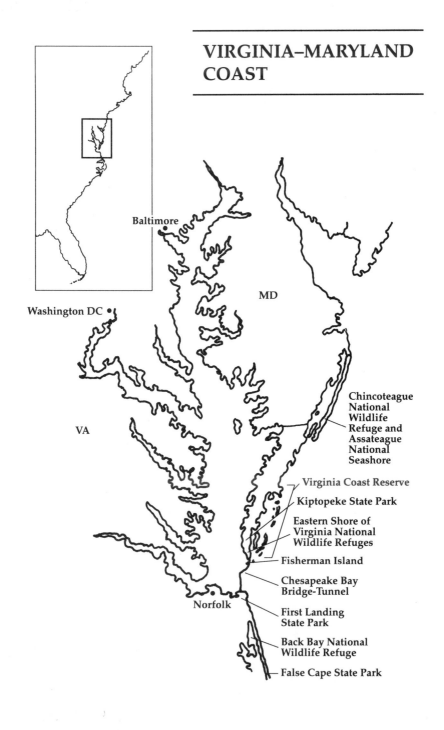

VIRGINIA–MARYLAND COAST

Baltimore

Washington DC

MD

VA

Chincoteague
National
Wildlife
Refuge and
Assateague
National
Seashore

Virginia Coast Reserve

Kiptopeke State Park

Eastern Shore of
Virginia National
Wildlife Refuges

Fisherman Island

Chesapeake Bay
Bridge-Tunnel

Norfolk

First Landing
State Park

Back Bay National
Wildlife Refuge

False Cape State Park

A NATURALIST'S GUIDE
TO THE VIRGINIA COAST

Curtis J. Badger
Illustrations by Cynthia Belcher

WITHDRAWN

University of Virginia Press
Charlottesville and London

University of Virginia Press
Originally published in 1996 by Stackpole Books
© 1996 by Curtis J. Badger
Printed in the United States of America on acid-free paper

First University of Virginia Press edition published 2004
ISBN 0-8139-2281-X (paper)

9 8 7 6 5 4 3 2 1

Library of Congress Cataloging-in-Publication Data

Badger, Curtis J.
  A naturalist's guide to the Virginia coast / Curtis J. Badger ;
illustrations by Cynthia Belcher.
     p. cm.
"Originally published in 1996 by Stackpole Books."
  ISBN 0-8139-2281-X (pbk. : alk. paper)
  1. Natural history—Virginia. 2. Coastal ecology—Virginia. I.
Title.
QH105.V8B325 2004
508.755—dc22
                                    2003018809

CONTENTS

Preface   vii

Acknowledgments   xi

The Processes: How Things Work

1 Islands and Lagoons—Change Is Constant   3

2 The Coastal People   11

3 Plants of the Coast   17

4 Life on the Tidal Flats   29

5 Birds of the Coast   38

6 Beachcombing   47

The Places: Islands, Bays, and Marshes

7 Back Bay National Wildlife Refuge
  and False Cape State Park   57

8 First Landing State Park   71

9 Chesapeake Bay Bridge-Tunnel   79

10 Fisherman Island and Eastern Shore of Virginia
   National Wildlife Refuges   83

11 Kiptopeke State Park   88

12 The Nature Conservancy's Virginia Coast Reserve   94

13 Chincoteague National Wildlife Refuge
   and Assateague National Seashore   103

PREFACE

One of my most memorable experiences in observing wildlife took place on the fifteenth floor of the Ramada Inn in Virginia Beach on a bitter January weekend not long ago. My wife Lynn and I spent the afternoon with binoculars and spotting scopes on the balcony of our oceanfront room, watching a huge flock of northern gannets dive for fish a few hundred yards beyond the empty beach and the thundering breakers.

Patrolling the ocean were thousands of gannets, magnificent white seabirds with black-tipped wings six feet across. They would soar and dive, soar and dive, sometimes disappearing behind the hillock of a large swell. We watched them all afternoon and then took the binoculars down to the restaurant, where we caught the twilight performance from a window table while dining on broiled flounder.

This is to say that memorable experiences in observing wildlife do not necessarily have to come in wilderness settings. Being a good naturalist has more to do with being an enthusiastic observer than traveling to distant wild places. It is more a matter of curiosity than of a need for adventure, a frame of mind rather than peculiarity of place.

Some people prefer their experiences with nature to be aided by various devices. That's why we have zoos, museums, interpretive programs, nature videos, and guidebooks. They shorten the learning curve, and they add a layer of comfort and safety when approaching a new and unknown world. You can learn about life on a tidal flat without actually getting your feet muddy. But many of us prefer to have muddy feet, and the truly inquisitive among us will watch a video about the tidal flats and then feel the need to get mud between our toes, to feel the steely chill of an incoming tide as it covers the flat and reawakens the grasses, worms, and clams that live there.

This book on the natural history of the Virginia coast is for everyone—those who watch gannets while dining on flounder, and those who walk the marshes and mudflats, enjoying the daily pulse of tides, the healthy suck of mud. I hope to incite your interest in this special place where the land meets the sea, to encourage you not only to watch the videos and attend the interpretive programs but also to get out there and get your feet muddy.

The Virginia coast is a wonderfully diverse place where you can dine in comfort while watching gannets as they dive for dinner or walk a wilderness beach for hours without seeing another soul. As such, Virginia offers a natural history experience for those of all levels of skill, interest, and inclination.

Virginia Beach is a popular and highly developed tourist city, but within its jurisdiction is First Landing State Park (formerly known as Seashore), an area of ancient cypress forests where Spanish moss hangs from the trees and migrating songbirds gather in spring and fall. A few miles south of Virginia Beach are Back Bay National Wildlife Refuge, which is home each winter to tens of thousands of waterfowl, and remote False Cape State Park.

Across the Chesapeake Bay are other national wildlife refuges—Fisherman Island, Eastern Shore of Virginia, and Chincoteague—plus the crown jewel of the coast, The Nature Conservancy's Virginia Coast Reserve. This fifty-thousand-acre sanctuary of fourteen barrier islands, marshes, and mainland is a coastal wilderness that remains today much as it was when the Europeans settled there in the 1620s.

The Virginia coast offers something for all—education

programs at museums, easy wildlife watching at numerous refuges, and a wilderness experience on Virginia's Eastern Shore. From classrooms to tidal flats, opportunities to learn about nature abound.

This guide is divided into two sections. The first deals with natural processes—how things work—and the second with special places on the coast that are accessible to the public.

The Virginia coast is typically composed of, from east to west, sandy barrier island beaches, dunes, shrub thickets, maritime forest, salt marshes, shallow bays and tidal flats, more salt marshes, and coastal fastland. These are the places discussed in the first section of this naturalist's guide. Chapters cover barrier island geology, the human history of the islands and coastal fastland, plants of the islands and marshes, life on the tidal flats, birds of the coast, and beachcombing. As an amateur naturalist who has an inordinate fondness for the barrier islands and salt marshes of the coast, I have included in the second section places that mean a great deal to me, for one reason or another. They range from Back Bay and False Cape in southeast Virginia near the North Carolina border to Assateague Island in the north, which is shared by Maryland and Virginia. In between the two lies a wealth of opportunities for naturalists—from the wilderness of an unmanipulated barrier island lagoon system on the Eastern Shore to formal programs on barrier island dynamics at the Virginia Museum of Marine Science in Virginia Beach.

In writing about various locations, I have tried to capture a sense of place. Obviously, attending an interpretive program with twenty other people at a wildlife refuge is quite different from canoeing a remote salt marsh stream alone. Both can be valuable experiences, depending on one's needs and motivation, and I have provided in each description a "wildness quotient," with one being the least wild and ten being the wildest, that should aid visitors in tailoring trips to their particular interests. I have also tried to incorporate some of the character of different places in my descriptions, to put into context the experience of observing and learning about nature. Observing a flock of black ducks from your car on a refuge impoundment is quite different from flushing black ducks while paddling your canoe in a tidal marsh. The ducks are the same, but the experience is different, and that's something I've tried to capture in this guide.

ACKNOWLEDGMENTS

I would like to thank the management and professional staff of the various state parks and wildlife refuges of the Virginia coast who gave me advice, showed me facilities, proofread manuscripts, and otherwise made life easier for me. Special thanks to Reese Lukei, who taught me a great deal about the Back Bay and False Cape area.

Thanks also to The Nature Conservancy's Virginia Coast Reserve and its director, John Hall, and director of research and education, Terry Thompson.

THE PROCESSES:
HOW THINGS WORK

1   ISLANDS AND LAGOONS— CHANGE IS CONSTANT

Stand on a barrier island beach on a breezy day and you can see the island change around you. Sand collects around a driftwood log and a small dune begins to build. Light, dry sand from atop another dune is swept away, tiny grains tumbling along the beach until they are trapped in the wind shadow of a hillock.

The surf, breaking at an angle to the beach, stirs up tons of sand, lifting it and sending it southward along the beach in what is called the alongshore current, or littoral drift. The sand will continue to travel in seawater until the current slows and it drops to the bottom, perhaps inside an inlet or at a beach structure such as a jetty or groin.

Barrier islands are in a constant state of change, a fact that is evident each time we place a towel on the beach, go swimming, and return a few minutes later to find the towel covered with sand. Barrier beaches are amoeba-like in that they constantly adapt to outside pressures. The wind scatters dunes and creates new ones; a northeast storm closes one inlet and opens another. In this way, the islands protect the mainland from storms, dissipating the energy as waves crash over their low, wide beaches.

Changes in the Virginia barrier islands can be seen on a daily basis and on a much broader timescale too. Older residents can tell you that a certain group of pilings, now in the ocean, was once part of a dock on the bay side of an island. Prior to a storm in the late summer of 1933, Assateague Island was part of a peninsula that extended southward from Fenwick Island, Delaware. The storm cut an inlet that now separates Assateague from Ocean City.

The sea level is rising, so the barrier islands of the coast are moving westward. This process has been going on for thousands of years at varying rates, as water stored in glaciers is slowly released.

Geologists say that there have been four major glaciations during the past million years of the earth's history. With each, ice and snow accumulated to great thicknesses and covered large parts of North America. With so much of the earth's moisture captured in ice, the sea level fell, only to rise again as the ice gradually melted.

Sea level rise means a gradual westward movement of the beaches, with dunes often forming in what was once a maritime forest.

Over a period of thousands of years, the sea has retreated eastward on the continental shelf at least fifty miles. It also has covered much of tidewater Virginia, inundating the state to near the fall line. When the sea level was low, the Delmarva Peninsula was actually a continuation of land west of the Chesapeake Bay, which at that time was the river valley of the Susquehanna.

During the last glaciation, the Eastern Shore was covered with a boreal forest of spruce and pine, much like those in central Canada today. The forest was bisected by numerous streams and rivers, which ran from what is now the spine of the peninsula to the sea, perhaps sixty miles eastward. The remnants of these rivers can be seen as underwater canyons and crevices extending from the contemporary coast all the way to the edge of the continental shelf.

The most recent glaciation, called the Wisconsin glacial stage, helped define the geology of the coast as we know it today. At the maximum extent of glaciation, some twenty thousand years ago, ice sheets covered North America from the Pole as far south as Long Island and north-central Pennsylvania. At that time, the shoreline of what we know as the Virginia coast was fifty to sixty miles east of where it is today. Core samplings taken from the offshore bottom include layers of salt marsh peat, indicating that there were salt marshes on the coast during that period.

Other samplings have turned up freshwater peat, with pollen of fir, spruce, pine, oak, water lily, and arrowhead. Using radiocarbon dating methods, scientists have examined peat remains and various fossils to establish a tentative chronology of the coast as the Wisconsin glacial period was on the wane. They estimate that 13,500 years ago, the area fifty miles east of the current coastline was covered with freshwater ponds and forest, with salt marshes apparently lying even farther eastward. But by 9,600 years ago, with the sea level rising, the area of freshwater ponds and forest had become an estuary.

So the subtle rise of the sea level we have today, estimated at one inch each decade, and the resultant westward migration of the barrier beaches are manifestations of a glacial stage that began approximately twenty thousand years ago. At some point, the tide will turn, the rise of the sea level will cease, and a reversal will begin.

How the Islands Were Formed

The barrier island lagoon system along Virginia's coast is the product of a slowly rising sea level. As the sea level rose, waves and wind formed a berm and beach ridge just landward of the surf zone. As the sea continued to rise, the land west of the beach ridge was flooded, and the ridge remained as a barrier island. So the lagoon system of shallow bays and salt marshes is a product of a rising sea level, as are the islands themselves.

In geological terms, the barrier islands and salt marshes are relatively new. The process began about five thousand years ago, when the rising sea began eating away at the exposed headlands, freeing sand and silt that would be carried by currents to form sandbars and eventually islands.

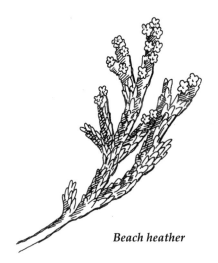

Beach heather

The rate of sea level rise slowed to approximately what it is today, allowing time for winds to build dunes, which were stabilized by grasses and, eventually, maritime forests.

As the sea level rose, it covered low areas of the islands, sending sand and silt into the lagoons behind them, helping to build tidal flats and salt marshes. In some areas, inlets were cut and were maintained by the scouring action of the tides.

A similar process continues today. Storm tides carry sand and silt across the islands and deposit them in the marshes on the island side of the lagoon, thus stabilizing the marshes and allowing them to grow. The marshes migrate westward, fed by the sediments of storm tides, and the beaches follow.

Inlets and Salt Marshes

Of interest to scientists are the location of inlets between the islands and the inlets' effect on the lagoon system. A typical island profile begins with the surf zone, then goes to a berm, a wide foredune area, and a substantial ridge of primary dunes, followed by shrubs or woodland, salt marsh, and then a lagoon system that separates the islands from the mainland.

Some lagoons on the Virginia coast are mainly shallow, open water, with some salt marsh fringing the upland west of the lagoon. Other lagoon systems include vast salt marshes, deep tidal creeks, tidal flats, and small areas of low upland called hammocks. It is likely that the location of ocean inlets determines the characteristics of the lagoon system that separates the island from the mainland.

For instance, islands that are broken regularly by inlets have more salt marsh, more flats, and more deep channels behind them than do islands that are unbroken. Examples of the former would be the Assawoman, Metomkin, Cedar, and Parramore Island areas of the Eastern Shore, where you can go from mainland to island without crossing significant wide water. The lagoon behind the north end of thirty-seven-mile-long Assateague Island, however, is mainly open water. Back Bay is an open-water, brackish lagoon behind the unbroken barrier spit of the Virginia Outer Banks.

Geologists believe that inlets allow sand and silt carried in the littoral drift to enter the lagoon and settle out as the velocity of the current drops when the narrow inlet enters the broader waters of a bay. Over time, tidal flats are created, which eventually become salt marshes, which eventually become shrub thickets or forest.

Of course, inlets are, by definition, temporary. The inlet separating Assateague from Ocean City was courtesy of a 1933 hurricane. A rock jetty was subsequently built on the north side of the inlet, and this captures sand from the alongshore

Typical barrier island topography includes, from right, the surf zone, berm, primary dunes, and shrub thicket or maritime forest.

current and keeps the inlet open. It also robs sand that might otherwise go to the north end of Assateague; as a result, north Assateague has accelerated its westward migration and has become very narrow, with none of the vast salt marshes usually associated with inlets. Assateague has, however, grown on its southern end, wrapping around Chincoteague Inlet in an area called The Hook, and sand is filling a lagoonal bay called Toms Cove and is building marshes in the southern portion of Chincoteague Bay.

Years ago, at least two other inlets broke Assateague Island, one near North Beach and the other at Green Run. Although the inlets have long been closed, it is interesting that in the lagoon where they were located there are significant salt marsh tracts, Tingle's Island and Middlemoor. Geologists believe that these marshes were fed by the inlets and are now diminishing in extent because they no longer receive sand and silt delivered by inlet currents.

Additionally, geologists believe that years ago Chincoteague was the barrier island along the coast here, and Assateague was farther north, the southern tip of a peninsula that begins on the Delaware coast. A nipped-off dune ridge on the north end of Chincoteague suggests that at one time an inlet might have cut through. It is known that since 1850 Assateague has been migrating southward, capturing what might have once been the Chincoteague coastline.

Productivity and Resiliency

The geological processes that have created and maintained the Virginia barrier island and lagoon system have given rise to one of the most productive natural systems on earth. These shallow waters, vast salt marshes, tidal flats, and forested upland support a remarkable diversity of life. The salt marsh has been called a great protein factory, a place where lush grasses

The salt marsh is a vast protein factory, with tidal waters rich in nutrients.

capture the energy of the sun and share it with the myriad creatures that depend on the bays and marshes for life.

The geology of the coast provides the structure, the ideal setting, for this to take place. In summer, the water is cloudy with tiny plankton. The tidal waters carry nutrients throughout the lagoon, supporting the growth of salt marsh plants and maintaining a salinity that is favorable to such creatures as clams, oysters, crabs, and fish.

It is perhaps ironic that a natural system that seems fragile and precariously balanced is based on geological processes that are in a constant state of change and can at times be violent. But change is part of the system; indeed, it is the only constant. It proves that this natural system is not only diverse and productive but also resilient.

2   THE COASTAL PEOPLE

Now and then, when I'm walking a barrier beach or salt marsh, I'll come across a stone tool—a scraper or arrowhead—and I'm reminded of the briefness of my stay here in this place and in this life. When it comes to the big picture, I'm just a blip on the screen.

These islands and marshes have been around for thousands of years, and hundreds of generations of humans have lived here. The person who used that stone scraper might have lived here before the time of Christ. He might have hunted this land when it was miles from the sea, when the glacial tide was still at an ebb.

Humans have been a component of the natural history of the Virginia coast for centuries. We are, after all, part of the food chain, and our activities have left their mark on the natural system.

The first coastal people were hunter-gatherers, predecessors of the powerful Powhatan tribe that ruled southeast Virginia at the time of European settlement. Little is known about them. On the coast, with a wealth of game and fish free for the taking, they probably did not engage in agriculture to a great extent. They did engage in commerce, though. The stone tools we find were probably made west or north of the coast, because there is little native rock here. Coastal Indians traded for them, using beads made of hard-shell clam (appropriately named *Mercenaria mercenaria*) as currency.

The first permanent English settlement was established at Jamestown in 1607, although Europeans had explored the coast before that. Like the native Americans, the Europeans found that the coastal waters and marshes held a wealth of fish and game. The barrier islands were also important for the making of salt, which was distilled from seawater. Salt works were established in the Back Bay area, on Smith and Mockhorn Islands at the tip of the Eastern Shore, and probably elsewhere.

The bays, creeks, and marshes of the coast provided fish, shellfish, wild game, salt, and various other necessities. Until federal law banned the practice, egg collecting was a popular rite of spring in coastal marshes. The eggs of gulls, clapper rails, whimbrels, and other birds were gathered, providing a welcome alternative to chicken eggs for breakfast. Whimbrel eggs were reported to be especially tasty. *Salicornia*, the tubular little salt marsh plant, was pickled in vinegar and spices and served as a relish.

There are tales all along the coast of pirates, treasures, sunken ships, and Revolutionary War skirmishes. No doubt a few of them are true. The remote barrier islands were attractive

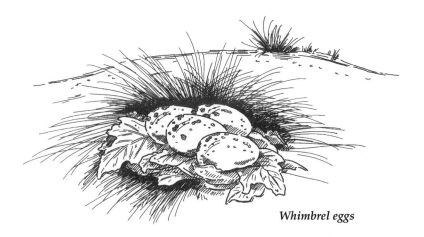

Whimbrel eggs

to people who, for one reason or another, wanted little contact with others. The islands and salt marsh hammocks also made good pastures, and most of the barrier islands had small communities of people who fished, farmed, looked after livestock, and did whatever else they could to make ends meet.

In the 1800s, the various islands on the coast were home to close to a thousand people. Wash Woods, in what is now False Cape State Park, had a population of about 300. The village of Broadwater, on Hog Island, was home to 250. Other islands had smaller communities, and many of them had schools, churches, and places of business and entertainment.

Most of the island people worked on the water, although there was fertile soil on many islands and people grew kitchen gardens and sold crops at market. The rising sea level and the westward migration of the beaches eventually covered the fertile soil with sand on most islands.

After the Civil War, the islands of the Virginia coast became nationally known among sportsmen. Hotels and sporting clubs were numerous, and they ranged from spartan shacks built on pilings in the marsh to lavish facilities with all the modern conveniences. Shipwrecks were frequent, and island residents often viewed them as serendipitous events, salvaging what they could of the cargo and the ship itself. Wrecks became less frequent in the mid-1800s when lighthouses were built and lifesaving stations were manned on most islands. The U.S. Coast Guard was later an active presence, but in the 1960s, the number of stations was reduced. The last barrier island station, Parramore, was closed in 1994 and its staff moved to the mainland town of Wachapreague.

Given the long-standing human presence in coastal Virginia, the ecosystem seems none the worse for wear. There is a major resort city, of course, and some barrier island and lagoon habi-

tat has been altered through projects to aid certain constituent species. But when viewed over the long term, most of these alterations are temporary.

It's important to keep in mind, I think, that humans are a part of the life cycle of the islands, bays, and salt marshes, and have been for thousands of years. This realization has changed the way we go about protecting natural resources. At one time, the standard method of protecting special places was to put up fences, post signs, and have armed, uniformed people patrolling them. That approach was limited and exclusionary and was not designed for long-term protection. In some instances, it became counterproductive as "protection" of these special places also drew people to them, damaging the area that happened to fall outside the jurisdiction of the "preserve."

Long-term protection of a vast natural resource such as the Virginia barrier islands and lagoon system is a matter of building partnerships rather than fences. The human element of natural history cannot be ignored, and any long-term protection plan must consider human needs as well as those of plants and other animals. The question is how to provide appropriate human use of the resource without damaging it.

The Nature Conservancy has been seeking answers to this question since the early 1990s, when it initiated its biosphere reserve program, which is based on the theory that humans can live in harmony with nature. The Virginia Coast Reserve was named a biosphere reserve, and it began enlisting various partners not only to help protect the resource but also to

Wax myrtle produces berries that are an important food source for many birds, especially the yellow-rumped warbler.

design appropriate uses of the resource to improve the quality of life of the people who are a part of it.

In the us-against-them, confrontational world of most conservation organizations, what the Conservancy was doing was akin to sleeping with the enemy. On Virginia's Eastern Shore, the Conservancy began working with business, industry, government, and local landowners to design a blueprint that would provide economic vitality within the context of resource protection. The result has been a move toward sustainable economic development, with an emphasis on the marketing of local food products and crafts and on low-impact tourism centered on the history, architecture, and natural resources of the area.

Ultimately, long-term protection of special places such as these islands, bays, and marshes is dependent on public attitude, and there has been a gradual change in the way that people perceive this resource. We are learning that protection is a good thing not just for plants and fish and birds but for humans as well. People, after all, are part of the system.

3   PLANTS OF THE COAST

The plants of the Virginia coast live in one of nature's least inviting environments. The water is salty, there is no shade and no protection from the winds, ice, and snow, and on a fairly regular basis, the plants are buffeted by storm tides that cover them completely. It takes a special plant to survive conditions like these, but the plants of the salt marshes and islands not only survive but thrive. Indeed, they are the building blocks of the entire barrier island lagoon system, the fuel that keeps the engines humming.

Salt Marsh Plants

The variety of plants in a coastal salt marsh is limited. Where salt water regularly covers the marsh, there are perhaps twelve species found with any regularity. Each has its place and its role to play. Indeed, the topography of the marsh is determined by the plants found there.

The dominant plants are the spartinas. *Spartina alterniflora*, salt marsh cordgrass, grows in the lowest areas and is regularly inundated by salt water. *Spartina patens*, salt meadow hay, is the predominant grass of the high marsh.

The spartinas are amazing plants. They have adapted to an environment that would quickly kill other grasses, and their life cycle drives the life of the salt marsh. In summer, salt marsh cordgrass stores the energy of the sun; in fall and winter, it collapses and decays, beginning a process of transferring the sun's energy to the countless tiny marsh animals that make up the lower rungs of the food chain.

Salt meadow hay has a similar life cycle, but the decaying process takes longer because the grass grows on the higher marsh and is not regularly swept away by the tides. Salt meadow hay lies in thick cowlicks in marshy meadows. If you're careful, you can reach under the current year's growth, raise it, and see the previous season's crop slowly decaying, its cowlick spiraling in a different direction. Some decaying hay is swept away by the tides, but most remains where it grew, helping to build the peat substrate on which the marsh grows.

The spartinas and other salt marsh plants are intriguing. How are they able to survive in an environment that would bring quick death to nearly any other plant? Interestingly, salt marsh cordgrass seems to thrive on the salt water of the estuary, growing tallest and thickest along the edges of creeks and bays where its roots are immersed twice daily, its stems washed by the flowing tides.

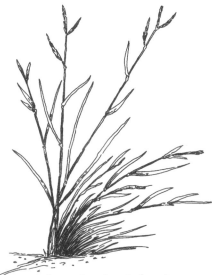

Salt meadow hay is found in the higher elevations of the salt marsh.

On the salt marsh, cordgrass is ubiquitous. Along the edges of creeks and bays, it grows in thick stands sometimes to heights of six feet. On the upper marsh, where tidal flow is limited, the grass is shorter, from about six inches to two or three feet, and it grows less dense, often with colonies of *Salicornia*, or saltwort. On the higher marsh, where the salt marsh joins fastland, cordgrass gives way to salt meadow hay and salt grass, which grow together in thick cowlicks.

The life of the entire barrier island lagoon community
begins here with these grasses
that form the basis of the food
chain, collecting the energy of
the sun in photosynthesis, and
later distributing it to myriad
creatures as the grasses are
broken down by bacteria. This
mixture of bacteria, epiphytic
algae, larvae, eggs, and the
cellulose particles of partially
digested spartina forms a nutrient-rich soup called detritus,
the life-giving concoction on
which many salt marsh creatures depend. This rich detritus
mixture is eaten by microscopic
crustaceans that live in the shallow water, by the filter-feeding
burrowing worms of the tidal
flats, by oysters, clams, mussels,
nematodes, snails, insect larvae,

Salicornia *is a small tubular*
plant common to the higher
marsh. There are three varieties
on the Virginia coast.

fiddler crabs, and small fish such as menhaden and mullet,
which either filter the nutrients from the water or ingest them
with bottom mud.

Clams burrow beneath the bottom and send up a pair of
siphons, one of which pulls detritus-rich seawater through
its digestive system while the other expels small nondigest-
ible particles and waste. Most of the filter-feeders consume
detritus in this manner, sucking the broth through hairlike
cilia, through membranes, or, in the case of the marsh mussel,
through a mesh of mucous threads covering its gills.

Fiddler crabs eat detritus by picking up gobs of it with their claws, then sorting out the digestible particles with six specially adapted legs that cover their mouths. The tiny legs are shaped like paddles and are covered with stiff bristles that sort the large particles of food from the small. The small particles are digested, but the larger pieces are temporarily stored in a predigestive chamber; when they accumulate, they are spit back into a claw and returned to the surface of the marsh.

The marsh periwinkle feeds on the lower stems of salt marsh cordgrass, scraping away algae and detritus that have collected on the plant.

The detritus eaters are preyed upon by animals higher on the food chain: larger fish, blue crabs, waterfowl, wading birds, raccoons, and other mammals. A clapper rail stalks the cordgrass marsh, spearing an unsuspecting periwinkle snail from a grass stem. A great blue heron waits patiently in a shallow gut, then surprises a passing killifish. An osprey circles over the open creek, dives, and comes up with a mullet in its talons. A fisherman drifts in a small boat along a tidal creek, hoping to entice a flounder with an offering of squid and minnows.

The salt marsh is one of the earth's most productive natural systems, producing an estimated three to six million tons of detritus per acre each year. But the remarkable thing about the marsh is that the spartina grasses are able to function at all, much less begin a process that gives life to creatures ranging from one-celled animals to humans. The salt water would literally suck the life out of less adapted plants, were they to find their way to the marsh. Through the process of osmosis, nature attempts to balance the concentration of particles suspended in water by moving a less concentrated solution through a membrane to a more concentrated one.

If a freshwater plant suddenly found itself in salt water, the water contained in the plant's cells would be drawn through the plant's membranes toward the more concentrated salt water until the concentrations became equal. In a very brief time, the freshwater contained in the plant would be removed, and the plant would die.

The spartinas have solved this problem by allowing a certain amount of salt to enter their cells, bringing the salt content of water within the plant to a slightly higher concentration than that of the surrounding seawater. In this manner, the osmotic pressure is reversed; instead of freshwater moving away from the plant cells, seawater attempts to enter, inflating the plant cells and giving them strength and resiliency.

The grasses are selective with regard to the salts they allow to enter, and they screen out those that might harm the plant. The most common sea salt, sodium chloride, is allowed to pass, as is a small amount of potassium, which is an important nutrient for the grass. The salts are screened by a cellulose membrane that covers the plant's roots. Excess and unneeded salts are concentrated on the membrane and are washed away by seawater and rain as it leeches into the soil. Other excess salts are secreted through glands on the upper surfaces of the leaves. On a dry summer day, a tiny coating of salt crystals makes the cordgrass leaves shimmer in the sunlight. The crystals did not dry on the leaves as seawater evaporated but instead came from within the plant as it attempted to maintain its perfect pitch of osmotic pressure.

The spartina, like most land plants, draws moisture from the soil as water evaporates from its leaves. The plant breathes in carbon dioxide, ingested through cells in its leaves called stomata, which open during the day when the plant is active and then close at night to conserve water. Water evaporates while the stomata are open during the day, and as it does the plant pulls water from the soil to replace it, much as someone might suck a soft drink through a straw. The water is transported through thin columns filled with spongy tissues called xylem, and the evaporative pressure placed on the water column helps give the plant strength.

Living in a saltwater environment is not the only challenge the spartinas must overcome. The plants live in a dense soil that is very low in oxygen, and they must compete for this scarce element with millions of bacteria and higher organisms that live in the upper layers of the soil. The grasses have solved their oxygen problem by adapting a series of air passages called intercalary canals, which transmit oxygen down to the roots, where it is needed. If you pull up a salt marsh cordgrass plant, you will usually see reddish mud adjacent to some of the roots. This is caused by oxygen reacting with iron sulfide in the soil to produce iron oxide—or rust.

So the spartinas survive in a hostile environment by using the salt that would kill other plants to their advantage, creating a positive osmotic pressure that inflates the plant and strengthens it. And while water is carried upward from the roots through the xylem, spartinas move oxygen molecules downward through intercalary canals. But although the cordgrasses have adapted several chemical and physical mechanisms that allow them to thrive on salt water and to feed oxygen to their roots, they still must overcome another problem presented by the estuary—the daily buffeting of the tides, as well as occasional violent storms.

The spartinas, especially salt marsh cordgrass, live in a physically demanding environment. The marsh has no windbreaks, so the breezes bend the slender stems at will. During storms, the ocean can breach the barrier islands and break directly upon the marsh, sending tons of water crashing down on the shafts of grass. Even on normal days, the twice-daily high tides flood the marsh, bending the grasses in a fast-moving current.

So cordgrass must first of all be solidly anchored, which it does by sending tough rhizomes through the muddy soil and interlocking root systems with other plants, finding strength not as individuals but as colonies of plants that survive or perish together. The shafts of the plants must also be resilient and tough, willing to bend but reluctant to break. Salt marsh cordgrass accomplishes this with the same mechanisms it uses to survive in salt water. By adjusting its osmotic pressure so that its cells are always fully inflated, the plant functions like a tire tube, able to withstand great shock before puncturing. And the thin column of water contained in the xylem, drawn constantly through the roots by evaporation taking place on the leaves, helps make the plant flexible but extremely strong.

The stems are also engineered for strength. Cut one off and you'll see a tube within a tube, precisely separated by cellulose spacers. The stems carry no water or gases; their only function is one of support, and they run all the way from the seed head down to the underground rhizomes.

The spartinas are a wonder of chemistry, physics, and structural engineering. Whereas most plants would wilt within hours of being placed in their environment, they thrive, and because of their remarkable adaptability, they have their particular part of the marsh nearly all to themselves. Saltwort, the

Cordgrass produces tough rhizomes that help stabilize the salt marsh.

only other plant common in the lower marsh, seems to complement cordgrass rather than compete with it. It is a tiny plant and seems at home growing among the thin stands of cordgrass away from the water's edge.

Sea oxeye is one of the most colorful plants of the salt marsh, with yellow blossoms that appear in late summer.

The plants define the topography of the lower tidal marsh. It is a precarious landscape, where only a few inches in elevation separate cordgrass from its smaller, finer cousins salt meadow hay and salt grass, which grow in the higher marsh, where the tides reach only during the peaks of the monthly cycles. Each plant has its niche, well defined and precise: salt marsh cordgrass on the lowest marshes, followed by salt meadow hay; the three species of saltwort found on the Virginia coast; salt grass, similar in appearance to salt meadow hay; sea lavender, with its tiny blue flowers in summer; sea oxeye, a striking, succulent plant with yellow flowers in summer and brown, prickly seed heads in winter; marsh elder; groundsel; and, on the lowest fastland, wax myrtle and cedar.

This range of salt marsh plant species occurs over a change in elevation of one foot or less, and subtle changes in sea level bring about dramatic differences in plant communities. Currently, the sea level is rising at a rate of about one inch per decade, and marshes dominated by salt meadow hay are gradually giving way to salt marsh cordgrass. Conversely, many tidal creeks and bays are becoming shallower because of siltation, and we see the emergence of cordgrass marshes in areas that were once tidal flats or bottom.

The salt marsh is a living ecosystem, and the plants that live there continuously adapt to changes in their environment, be they changes of season or sea level or interruption by humans. Marsh plants are at once fragile and resilient, specialized and opportunistic. And they possess a beauty that changes as the seasons change. An expansive salt marsh presents an enduring landscape, a signature of the Virginia coast.

Beach Plants

Like the salt marsh, the beaches and dunes of the barrier islands constitute a harsh environment where only a few well-adapted plants can survive. Consider the conditions. Fertile soil is covered by a constantly shifting layer of sand. During storms, ocean breakers can drop tons of water on dune plants, scouring away the sand around them and exposing their roots and rhizomes to the air. Even on good days, the air is filled with salt picked up by the breezes from breaking surf. The plants that survive here have evolved some special adaptations to help them fill this particular niche in coastal life. Some, such as beach grass and sea oats, seem to thrive in this hostile environment, just as the spartinas do on the salt marsh.

American beach grass, *Ammophila breviligulata*, has a vertical rhizome, or underground stem, that sometimes reaches thirty to forty feet beneath the apex of a dune. If sand covers a mature stand of beach grass, it sends the rhizome higher until it reaches the surface. The roots of the plant extend down to the upper areas of the water table. If you visit a barrier beach after a storm has passed and cut away a portion of a dune, you can see the rhizomes and clumps of the plant at various levels where mature grass once grew.

Beach plants begin growing along the wrack line seaward of the primary dunes. Wrack is deposited by the surf at the highest tides and consists of decaying cordgrass, remains of submerged vegetation and other plant material, mermaid's purses (skate egg casings), and various other flotsam, including cans and bottles deposited overboard by unthinking humans and, for some curious reason, numerous lightbulbs.

The wrack line, with the organic matter it carries, provides the first habitable area on the beach for plant growth. Seeds, sometimes carried to the beach as part of the wrack, get the chance to germinate. Few make it, but those that do are well adapted to the environment. Sea rocket, *Cakile edentula*, has succulent, fleshy stems that help the plant store water; it grows low to the ground, allowing it to avoid the drying effects of wind and take advantage of the protection of the wrack. Russian thistle and cocklebur are often found with sea rocket between the wrack line and the primary dune.

Atop the primary dune, beach grass is the predominant plant. Indeed, its rhizome system and its ability to tolerate sand accretion help build and stabilize primary dunes. In areas where there are man-made dunes, such as Assateague and Back Bay, beach grass is planted to help stabilize the dunes and promote accretion.

Sea oat, *Uniola paniculata*, is a tall (three to six feet) and stately dune plant whose seed head turns a bronze-yellow in the fall. Like beach grass, it has adapted to wind, salt spray, and accreting sand. On the Virginia coast, it is found primarily in the southern portions. Other plants of the primary dunes include beach heather, especially in the northern portions, and sandbur.

Landward of the primary dunes, plants find shelter from the onshore wind and salt spray. The number of species thus increases, but it is still a harsh environment, and the plants found there have developed special ways to adapt to it. Some, such as the prickly pear cactus, are succulents, able to store water to counter the drying effects of a desert-like environment. Others, such as the bayberry and wax myrtle, have a waxy coating to protect them from salt spray. Beach heather is covered with tiny white hairs that insulate it from the sun's heat and reflect sunlight.

Even upland trees such as loblolly pine and live oak are shaped by the island environment. Many are dwarfed or pruned by the effects of wind and salt spray.

Landward of the primary dune is a shrub thicket, perhaps lower secondary dunes, and in some cases a maritime forest. Westward of the forest is a salt marsh, and then the bays, flats, and creeks that separate the island portion of the lagoon system from the mainland portion.

The primary plants of the shrub thicket are the myricas. *Myrica pensylvanica* is known locally as bayberry. It is a deciduous shrub with fragrant leaves and gray berries favored by many songbird species. On the Virginia coast, bayberry is mixed with wax myrtle, *Myrica cerifera*, and biologists believe that the plants have hybridized, making positive identification difficult. Wax myrtle is an evergreen and, in general, has narrower leaves and smaller fruits than bayberry. Neither produces the bay leaf used to season stews and marinades. That would be the red bay, *Persea borbonia*, a tree of the southern maritime forest. In the past, the gray fruits of the myricas were used to make scented candles.

Other plants of the shrublands include poison ivy, beach heather, sandbur, switchgrass, and grasses associated with the high marsh, such as salt meadow hay. Beach plum grows in the northern portion of the coast and can be seen along the dune trail at Assateague National Seashore.

On some barrier islands, the shrub thicket gives way to a maritime forest, most of which was created when pioneer plants such as loblolly pine and live oak took root and survived, thanks to the protection of the shrub thicket. In such forests, common plants include greenbrier, poison ivy, wild black cherry, red cedar, American holly, fox grape, and sassafras.

Nearly all the plants of the shrub thicket and maritime forest are of value to wildlife. The fruits are eaten by migrating birds and residents alike, and the thick cover provides protection from predators such as sharp-shinned and Cooper's hawks. Deer, raccoon, opossum, and numerous other mammals also live in the shrubland and forest, and the endangered Delmarva fox squirrel is found in the old-growth areas of Chincoteague National Wildlife Refuge as well as on a mainland farm owned by The Nature Conservancy.

The mainland is as integral to the barrier island lagoon system as are the islands, dunes, and marshes. After all, the lagoon system is part of the mainland watershed, and events that take place along mainland creeks and streams eventually have an effect on the lagoon system. For this reason, The Nature Conservancy and other concerned landowners are recommending land-use policies that steer intensive or inappropriate development away from the waterfront and toward areas where the impact on the natural system will be minimized.

4   LIFE ON THE TIDAL FLATS

The most underappreciated natural system of the barrier island lagoon system of the Virginia coast is the tidal flat. For one thing, we don't quite know what to make of it. It's not marshland; there are no grasses growing on it. Neither is it beach; we're not tempted to spread out a towel and lie down on it.

A tidal flat is essentially a broad expanse of bay bottom where the water is so shallow that the flat is exposed at low tide. This phenomenon has some interesting implications. Twice each day, we get to see the bay bottom uncovered. That is, all the submerged plants and animals normally hidden by water are in full view. Many are in hiding, but if we search carefully we can find them. Low tide on a flat gives us a chance to be hunter-gatherers. We can go clamming; we can gather oysters. Like the oystercatchers and whimbrels that share the flat with us, we go in search of good things to eat.

To the uninitiated, the tidal flat may seem rather unremarkable and uninviting. From a distance, it appears barren; the birds gathered on it are the only signs of life. The footing appears tenuous; the surface is slick with wet mud. But the birds that gather on an exposed flat are there for a reason. Dinner is served.

Get out of the boat, wade over to the flat, and take a good look. That barren piece of bay bottom is full of life. There are mud snails and ribbed mussels growing in clumps. Oysters attach themselves to a hard substrate and filter nutrients from the water. Clams burrow beneath the surface and suck seawater through a siphon. There are shallow depressions

The ribbon worm is one of the many burrowing creatures that live on the tidal flats.

where, during high tide, a cow-nosed skake dug out a clam, crushed its shell, and ate it. There are green algae and slender red grasses, which now appear lifeless but will revive with the incoming tide. Worms burrow beneath the surface of the flat, leaving tiny holes as evidence. A whimbrel probes for them with its long, down-curved beak.

The Hard-Shell Clam

One of the creatures best adapted to the tidal flat is the hard-shell clam, or quahog. It is also the best known of the denizens of the flat—after all, clams make wonderful chowder, fritters, and linguine sauce. The clam hides itself well, however. It burrows beneath the surface and sends up two siphons, one for feeding and the other for expelling waste. You could walk right by a clam and not know that it was there. But those of us who enjoy the occasional bowl of chowder have learned to look for clam sign, the keyhole and waste midden left by the siphon. If we find them, we usually have ourselves a clam.

For a creature seldom seen outside a seafood shop, the clam lives a complex and colorful life. Many clams undergo a sex change at some point in their lives. Young clams are all functional males, but their permanent sexual identities are not yet determined. As the clams mature, they become male or female at about a one-to-one ratio.

The clam feeds by filtering phytoplankton, bacteria, detritus, and dissolved organic material from seawater. The incurrent siphon, which brings in nutrients, has tiny tentacles along its rim that sort out possible food particles. The tentacles act as the off-on switch for the siphon. When there are plenty of nutrients suspended in the current, the tentacles tell the clam to go into the feeding mode; if the seawater is clouded with suspended particles of sand, mud, and other large debris, the tentacles shut the system down.

The clam's digestive system also plays a role in reproduction. When the water temperature rises in the spring, male clams release semen through their feeding siphons. The semen

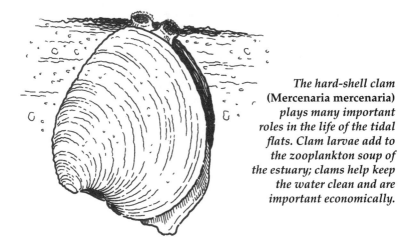

The hard-shell clam **(Mercenaria mercenaria)** *plays many important roles in the life of the tidal flats. Clam larvae add to the zooplankton soup of the estuary; clams help keep the water clean and are important economically.*

is spread over the flat by the currents and stimulates the females to release eggs, which they expel through their excurrent siphons. The eggs float freely in the current and are eventually attacked by spermatozoa, forming larvae.

Clam larvae float freely in the seawater, forming a vital part of the detritus and zooplankton soup of the estuary. After twelve to fourteen days, the larvae that survive begin their metamorphosis into seed clams. The shell thickens and a gland develops that secretes a tough thread, enabling the seed clam to anchor itself on the substrate. The tiny clam does not burrow at this stage but attaches itself to sand grains, small rocks, or shells with its thread. The attachment is not permanent; the clam can sever its link and move on to habitat that is more to its liking.

What the seed clams are looking for at this point in their young lives is water of proper salinity and a bottom that will be a good home for an adult clam. Clams grow best in seawater that contains about twenty to thirty-five parts per thousand of salt. In fact, the larval clam does not begin its metamorphosis to seed clam unless the salinity is at least eighteen to twenty parts per thousand, ensuring that the seed clam will not set in an area where the salinity is unsuitable for adults.

Clams also prefer a bottom substrate of sand or mud, and this is what the larval clam or seed clam looks for. The clam's favorite habitat is a sandy or muddy bottom in a shallow estuary where the current moves the water at a fairly leisurely pace. Clams don't like the fast-moving water of inlets, nor do they like turbid waters where the bottom has been disturbed. Although they feed on suspended food particles, excessive turbidity can clog the filtering system and eventually kill the clam.

The hard-shell clam, like the spartina grasses, is vital to the life of the lagoon. As filter-feeders, clams help clean the water, and their remarkable fecundity contributes to the rich life of the seaside bays. Mature female clams can produce more than fifty million eggs per season. Of course, only a small percentage of the eggs survive to become adult clams. The eggs, spermatozoa, and clam larvae all become part of the zooplankton carried by the currents through the lagoon, which in summer provides a nutrient-rich soup for a wide variety of animals. Scientists say that in a shallow seaside estuary during the summer months, there can be as many as thirty million clam larvae per square meter.

Most of the larvae are eaten by fish, crabs, birds, and other mollusks. Even clams eat their own eggs and larvae by filtering them out of seawater. The clam's vulnerability decreases as it outgrows this army of predators. Once the clam becomes an adult and burrows into the bottom, the predators become fairly specific. Mud crabs, blue crabs, and green crabs dig clams out of the sediment and crush the smaller shells with their claws and chip off the edges of larger shells.

Hairy sea cucumber

*The large claw of the male fiddler
crab is used to attract female fiddlers during mating.*

Several mollusks also feed on adult clams. Oyster drills and moon snails drill holes in the shells and remove the clam's tissues. Whelks chip off the edges of the clam's shell, then insert their proboscises through the opening and eat the living tissue. The sea star pulls the shells of the clam apart and inserts its stomach into the cavity, digesting the contents.

I prefer my clams cooked in their own salty broth, along with some diced potatoes, onions, and black pepper. On a cool fall evening, warmed by this rich chowder, I'm reminded how important tidal flats are.

How to Catch a Clam

There are three ways to catch clams: signing, raking, and treading.

Signing clams, as explained above, is done at low tide when the flat is exposed. You bend over and carefully inspect the surface of the flat. What you are looking for is a keyhole and with it the tiny threads of clam scat, each perhaps one-eighth of an inch long. Scratch around with a clam pick (available at most local sporting goods stores), and you should feel the rocklike presence of a clam. If not, keep searching.

The problem is, tidal flats are home to many creatures that burrow beneath the surface and leave holes that look like clam sign. And sometimes the clams simply don't make sign; they haven't been feeding or defecating. At such times, one turns to the clam rake, a tool that looks like a metal garden rake with extended tines. Using a clam rake requires a strong back and, I'm tempted to say, a weak mind. It's hard work. You pull the rake across the flat as if you were raking leaves, pressing down on it so the tines sink clam-deep into the bottom. When you hit a clam you'll hear the chalk-on-blackboard squeak of metal on calcium. Use the rake to pry the clam from the mud.

Treading is done in shallow water, and it's like doing the twist. You move your feet around until they settle slightly

Green fleece is one of the seldom-seen plants of the tidal flat.

into the bottom and can detect the rocky presence of a clam. Light-soled shoes such as nylon mesh water shoes are good for treading. Old-timers created their own treading shoes by making socks from tough, flannel material.

What to Do with a Clam Once You Get It

Clams are hard to open. Herring gulls dig them out of the flats, fly them to the nearest paved road, and drop them from a height of about fifty feet. That usually does it.

Lacking the gift of flight, humans have an adaptation called the oyster knife, an instrument with a strong, slender blade and a palm-sized wooden handle. The clam is vulnerable at one point—a spot just above the hinge. If considerable pressure is applied to the knife at that point, the blade will enter and the two strong muscles holding the shells together can be cut.

I prefer to put the clams in the freezer overnight. By the following day, they will open easily, and all the wonderful clam juice can be saved. This method is safer, lessening the possibility of poking yourself with the oyster knife. And because the clams open easily, there is less likelihood of getting bits and pieces of shell in with the meat.

There are many good ways to prepare clams, and usually the simplest is best. One of my favorites is Eastern Shore–style clam chowder, in which neither tomato nor cream is allowed. I dice two pieces of bacon, brown them in a large pot, then add a large onion chopped fine, three or four large diced potatoes, a dozen large clams that have been coarsely chopped, the juice that came with them, and enough water to make a proper chowder. Ground black pepper is added, but not salt. Clams grow in water that is plenty salty.

Another favorite recipe of mine is to brown four or five chopped garlic cloves in olive oil, then add a dozen chopped clams, clam juice, and fresh parsley. This is served over linguine. Garnish with a few steamed littleneck clams.

Clam fritters are made from a batter of a dozen large chopped clams, the clam juice, a chopped onion, one egg, half a cup of flour, one and a half teaspoons of baking powder, half a teaspoon of baking soda, and a little black pepper. The fritters are fried in hot oil until they are golden brown.

5   BIRDS OF THE COAST

When most people think of coastal birds, they think of ducks, geese, and long-legged wading birds such as herons and egrets. That's understandable. Most of the natural areas on the coast that are widely visited by the public are home to waterfowl and wading birds. Visit Chincoteague or Back Bay, as more than a million people do each year, and you go home with vivid impressions of Canada geese and great blue herons. But the bird life of the coast is much more varied than that, ranging from birds normally associated with water to colorful woodland warblers that have a decidedly tropical look. The checklist published by Chincoteague National Wildlife Refuge names more than three hundred species that can be spotted there.

The Canada goose is a resident bird on the Virginia coast.

At Chincoteague and Back Bay, waterfowl and wading birds are easy to see; you don't even have to leave the comfort of your car. But please park that car, put on your walking shoes, and get out into the woods, especially in spring and fall, when the songbird migration is at its peak. Only then will you appreciate the remarkable diversity of bird life on the coast.

The great blue heron can be found along shallow tidal creeks stalking small fish and crustaceans.

I know. There are mosquitoes out there. There's the possibility of ticks and chiggers, perhaps even snakes. So put on a long-sleeved shirt, tuck your pant legs into your boots, baste yourself with insect repellent, and get out there. It will be worth it.

Although wildlife refuges on the coast were built with waterfowl in mind, most of them support a healthy songbird population. Refuge managers have built hiking paths—many of which are paved or made of boardwalk—through wooded areas and thickets where the birds congregate. Assateague Island, Kiptopeke, Back Bay, False Cape, and First Landing are all excellent places to see migrating songbirds, and the trails make viewing easy. Bring your binoculars, field guides, and insect repellent, and learn about an aspect of bird life that many coastal residents are unaware of.

The importance of the coastal corridor for migrating waterfowl has long been recognized, but a study completed in 1993 found that the area was equally important for Neotropical migrant songbirds—the warblers, tanagers, vireos, and others that nest in the northern United States and Canada and spend their winters in the tropics. The Neotropical Migratory Songbird Coastal Corridor Study, with funding from both private and public sources, examined migrating birds and the habitat they used in New Jersey, Delaware, Maryland, and Virginia over a period of two years. Among the findings: birds are more abundant within a mile of the coast than farther inland, and migratory songbirds are more abundant on barrier islands than on the coastal mainland.

Ornithologists say that the populations of most Neotropical songbirds are down, and the conventional wisdom was that the clear-cutting of tropical rain forests in their winter range was the culprit. But this study shed new light on the importance of the migratory corridor and the need for a forested byway to provide the birds with food, shelter, and protection from predators. The study concluded that development along the coast, and the forest fragmentation that goes with it, could be as injurious to these birds as rain forest destruction. Fortunately, on the Virginia coast, this forested corridor is relatively intact, with a chain of refuges, parks, and The Nature Conser-

Migratory songbirds, such as this yellow-rumped warbler, need a forested corridor along the coast for their travels.

*Black ducks
feed in shallow ponds
and creeks of the salt marsh.*

vancy's Virginia Coast Reserve providing a protected travel-way along the coast, where the birds apparently prefer to be.

The Seasons of Birds

The Virginia coast is used by many migrating birds, not just the Neotropical migrant songbirds. Ducks and geese arrive in the fall and spend the winter unless a hard freeze drives them farther south. Shorebirds move northward in great numbers in

*Brant gather in large
flocks on the tidal flats
in winter, feeding on the
submerged vegetation.*

41

early spring and then return south in late summer. Songbirds pass through in May and October. For Canada geese, warblers, hummingbirds, and everything in between, the coast of Virginia is nature's own interstate highway, complete with rest stops and restaurants.

For those of us interested in birds, there are no dull seasons on the coast. In the earliest months of the year, there are ducks and geese on the impoundments at the wildlife refuges. The inshore ocean waters have thousands of sea ducks and pelagic birds such as northern gannets. At the Chesapeake Bay Bridge-Tunnel, the rock islands are surrounded by scoters, old-squaws, red-breasted mergansers, cormorants, and eiders. Great flocks of gulls congregate, and uncommon species can often be seen.

In early spring the shorebirds move through. A favorite activity of mine is to ride the back roads after a heavy rain and scan the farm fields with a spotting scope. There may be black-bellied plovers, sandpipers, yellowlegs, and many other species. If there is standing water, there are often dabbling ducks as well.

The endangered piping plover nests in shell litter on barrier island beaches.

The common tern nests in
colonies on barrier island beaches.

In April and May, the songbird migration is at its peak.
Barrier island beaches get their annual visits from terns, skimmers, brown pelicans, and piping plovers, all of which nest
here. Gulls and rails nest in the upper marshes, and herons,
egrets, and glossy ibises congregate in noisy colonies in wooded hammocks on the marsh. Ospreys nest in pine snags, on
channel markers, or on special platforms constructed for them.

By the time the nesting season is waning, the shorebirds are
moving back through, with the greatest migration occurring in
late July and August. Any shallow waterway with tidal flats is
a good place to see them.

American redstarts can be found
in maritime forests in spring and
fall during migrations.

43

In September, the movement of Neotropical songbirds begins as they leave their nesting areas in the north and head south along well-used routes. The early migration features a wide variety of birds—American redstarts, vireos, common yellowthroats, yellow warblers, Connecticut warblers, and many more. Later, by the end of October, there are thousands of yellow-rumped warblers, most of which spend the winter.

Not coincidentally, the fall arrival of songbirds is accompanied by great flocks of hawks. Kestrels suddenly show up on fences and power lines, northern harriers patrol the salt marsh, and the thickets and forests are hunted by Cooper's and sharp-shinned hawks, the major predators of songbirds. Peregrine falcons and merlins pass overhead as they follow the barrier island chain southward. Suddenly, the laughing gulls are gone and ring-billed gulls take their place.

This ever-changing kaleidoscope of bird life adds color and drama to the neighborhood, to the resident population of wrens, cardinals, towhees, chickadees,

The northern harrier, a common winter resident, can often be seen hunting the upper marsh and farm fields.

nuthatches, blue jays, titmice, and all the other birds that may be considered standard fare. The intriguing thing about coastal Virginia is that when you get out on the water or in the woods and salt marshes, you never know what you're going to see.

Best Places for Birds

For warblers and other Neotropical migrants: Kiptopeke State Park and Eastern Shore of Virginia National Wildlife Refuge. The banding station at Kiptopeke operates daily in September and October. Birds tend to gather on the tip of the Eastern Shore peninsula before crossing Chesapeake Bay. Also, the woodland trails at Chincoteague National Wildlife Refuge, Life of the Forest Trail at Assateague National Seashore in Maryland, the maritime forest at False Cape, and the various trails at First Landing State Park.

Peregrine falcons are seen frequently in the fall from the hawk observatory at Kiptopeke.

*Black skimmers are
common summer residents
and nest in colonies on undisturbed
beaches, such as those of the Virginia Coast Reserve.*

For waterfowl and wading birds: Chincoteague National Wildlife Refuge, Back Bay National Wildlife Refuge, and the Virginia Coast Reserve.

For sea ducks and pelagic species: Chesapeake Bay Bridge-Tunnel.

For shorebirds: Tidal flats of the Virginia Coast Reserve and shallow impoundments at Chincoteague and Back Bay National Wildlife Refuges.

6   BEACHCOMBING

The keyhole limpet looks like something from outer space, perhaps something from ancient Egypt. It could be a miniature spaceship, a time capsule capable of touring the galaxies. Or it could be a miniature version of a great Egyptian temple, a monument to gifted ancient architects.

Actually, the keyhole limpet is a seashell, and not a particularly flashy example at that, until you study it closely. The limpet is an oval shell an inch or two long, and it is shaped like a mountain, or perhaps a volcano, since it has an opening in its peak.

There are all sorts of limpets, ranging in color from pearly white to green to blue, and they are found on both coasts. The limpets found here on Virginia's beaches are usually cone shaped, with a row of file-like ridges running around the shell.

Viewed with a small magnifier, the limpet looks like something from *Star Wars*, a great traveling city encompassed in a shapely dome of calcium. Actually, the limpets we find on our beaches were once the homes of tiny mollusks, little marine invertebrates that cling to rocks and tree roots along the coast. As with most of the seashells we find locally, the animal that occupied the dwelling has long since checked out.

Every trip we take to the beach results in a few additions to an informal shell collection that, by the end of summer, dominates our back porch. My wife Lynn, son Tom, and I became interested in shells simply because we thought that they had pleasing shapes or colors. Soon we bought a field guide and began to identify our limpets, ceriths, moon shells, cockles, and arks. We learned to tell the difference between a channeled whelk and a knobbed whelk. We are not shell experts by any stretch of the imagination, but we enjoy our collection for a number of reasons, not the least of which is that it encourages us to spend our weekends hiking the beach.

Shell collecting is an inexpensive hobby, requiring only a good field guide, a collecting bag, and a willingness to walk. Our basic outfit consists of a fanny pack, an Audubon *Field Guide to North American Shells*, and the Peterson *Atlantic Seashore* field guide by Kenneth L. Gosner, which covers not only shells but also worms, seaweeds, crabs, and other creatures one might find stranded at the high-tide mark.

Virginia beaches have a wide variety of shells, ranging from large sea clam shells to tiny whelks smaller than the nail of your pinkie. In addition to limpets, you can find razor clams, pale orange arks, cockles, moon snails, worm shells, augers, ceriths, periwinkles, scallops, and fragile jingle shells. Most local beaches also have sand dollars, which are not actually shells but the calcified remains of an animal called an echinoid, which is related to the sea urchin.

Along the berm of the beach you can find glossy black skate

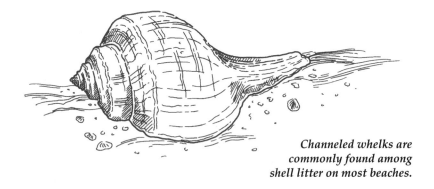

Channeled whelks are commonly found among shell litter on most beaches.

48

The blood ark is found on beaches along the entire Virginia coast.

egg casings, called mermaid's purses. The casings have been split open and their occupants have departed, presumably to begin feeding on the small fish and shrimp of the estuary.

You can also find egg casings of channeled and knobbed whelks; each case, about the size of a quarter, is attached to the other by a stout membrane, and from a distance they look like the spent skin of a snake. Some strings of egg casings may be two feet or more in length, and each translucent compartment holds, or held, dozens of miniature whelks. The casing of the knobbed whelk has a flat edge, and the edge of the channeled whelk casing is sharp. Now and then, if you slice open a casing with a knife, you can find a few tiny whelk shells inside, homes of the few animals that did not make it. But mostly the casings are filled with sand, which they picked up while tumbling around in the surf.

You are also likely to find the remains of sea turtles, bottle-nosed dolphins, and perhaps even whales. On a recent hike we found a turtle leg bone and a well-preserved skull and vertebra from a dolphin. It is illegal, however, to collect the remains of marine mammals, so these stayed on the beach.

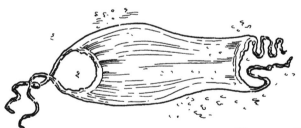

The mermaid's purse, actually the egg casing of a skate, is found on the beach and in marshes.

49

The whelk egg casing looks from a distance like a snake skin. Sometimes tiny whelks can be found in the spent compartments.

Underlying our fascination with seashells is the realization that the relics we find on the beach are symbols of the complex and mysterious life of marine invertebrates. Indeed, what we find on the beach is the remnant of marine life, the final chapter in the biographies of limpets, ceriths, arks, and other strange creatures.

Walk a beach after the passage of a northeast storm, and all manner of treasures may be found. Many shells, of course, but perhaps fossilized bone, bits of coral, interesting driftwood, and maybe even Indian artifacts. Once I found a fossilized inner ear bone of a whale lying at the base of a dune, washed up by a recent storm. It looked at first like a small, misshapen human skull. Then it looked like a giant tooth. An anthropologist from the Smithsonian Institution explained what it was. He gave me a diagram of the whale skull and highlighted the inner ear bone with a yellow marker.

Twelve thousand years ago, forest grew on what is now ocean floor. The barrier beaches and salt marshes were fifty or sixty miles east of here, and prehistoric creatures grazed on ancient grasses where we now fish for tuna. It tickles the imagination to know that a northeast storm could dislodge some wonderful artifact and send it to shore.

But such finds are rare. Mostly we come across common treasures: jingle shells, limpets, cockles, moon snails, arks, clams, scallops, and tiny snails such as wentletraps and ceriths. Jingle shells are among my favorites. Pick up a few and put them in your pocket and they jingle like loose change.

The jingle shell is related to the razor clam.

When wet with seawater, they glitter like shiny coins. Some are white, some orange, some nearly black. They are related to razor clams, the long, thin bivalves shaped like straight razors.

Find a beach devoid of humans, sit down for a while, and watch what goes on around you. You'll soon learn what a busy place it can be.

In May, terns, skimmers, and plovers nest in the shell litter beyond the berm of the beach. Sea turtles lumber ashore at

Holes dug just above the berm of the beach probably are the homes of ghost crabs.

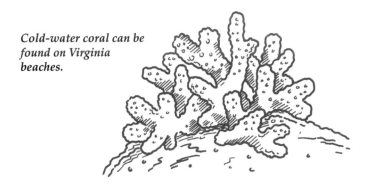

Cold-water coral can be found on Virginia beaches.

night and laboriously dig cavities in the sand in which they deposit dozens of leathery eggs. Predators are at work. A fish crow digs up the turtle eggs as soon as the exhausted mother disappears at dawn into the breakers. A great black-backed gull steals a tern chick. A fox raids a plover nest. A ghost crab invades a skimmer nest.

The beach, like other natural communities, is filled with daily dramas, the life-and-death struggles of individual animals to live and to reproduce. There are successes and failures. Helpless chicks are attacked by predators; a northeaster wipes

The scallop shell is noted by its two "wings" where the shells are hinged.

out a nesting colony. But the parent birds will nest again, and eventually the fledglings will evade the predators and join the fall flight to southern beaches.

By summer's end, our back porch is filled with island treasures. We have dozens of keyhole and slipper limpets, bits of coral, and lacy little stones that are actually colonies of tiny animals called bryozoans, which often build their com-

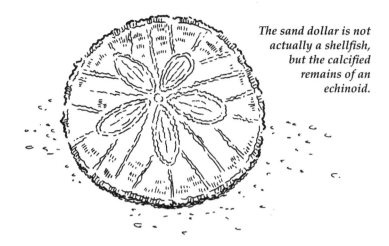

The sand dollar is not actually a shellfish, but the calcified remains of an echinoid.

munities around a pebble or shell. Large clam shells or the shells of sea scallops are put to use in the kitchen as individual serving dishes for deviled crab or clam. There are sand dollars, the purple-specked shells of lady crabs, an unidentified fossilized bone, a rotting plank from a wreck, and the jagged tail of a horseshoe crab.

These things will stay on the porch for an undetermined amount of time, and eventually they will disappear. Sand dollars disintegrate, the rotting plank completes its decay, the various other bits of beach detritus fall victim to various cleanups. By spring they will all be gone, but by then it will be time to start again, to get out on the beach for the first time and see what the winter might have delivered.

THE PLACES:
ISLANDS, BAYS, AND
MARSHES

7   BACK BAY NATIONAL WILDLIFE REFUGE AND FALSE CAPE STATE PARK

Head south on Pacific Avenue in Virginia Beach, cross Rudee Inlet, follow General Booth Boulevard to Princess Anne Road, take a left at the light, and begin traveling back in time.

Once you pass the shopping malls and subdivisions, the landscape reverts to cornfields and country churches, vegetable stands where in July you can get a dozen ears of Silver Queen corn so fresh and sweet it is sinful. It is southeast Virginia as it was a generation ago, a verdant landscape of fertile soil, quiet waters, and few people.

Turn left on Sandbridge Road and in a few miles you will see what Virginia Beach might have been like in the 1930s, before the condos and high-rise hotels. Weathered cottages perch on thick pilings, awaiting the next northeaster. Two-lane roads crisscross behind what remains of the dune line. There are a few stores and restaurants here in Sandbridge, but mainly there are vacation homes.

If you turn right on Sandpiper Road, the main street in Sandbridge, you will end up at Back Bay National Wildlife Refuge. If you cross the dunes and walk out onto the beach at Back Bay and look back north, you can see the beach moving.

In the distance are the high-rises of Virginia Beach, and in the middle ground are the summer residences of Sandbridge. The beach here is shaped like a horseshoe, with Virginia Beach and Back Bay being the points. Unfortunately, Sandbridge is at the bottom curve of the shoe, and with each storm the beach moves farther westward, progressively assuming its U-shape. Property has been destroyed, and debate goes on regarding whether and how various levels of government should do battle with a migrating beachline.

Reese Lukei, a naturalist who has spent his fifty-some years studying the Back Bay area, predicts that Sandbridge will one day become an inlet and that a bridge will be needed to connect Virginia Beach with Back Bay and False Cape. Lukei may or may not be right, but when you stand on the beach at Back Bay and look north, one fact of nature is emphatically driven home: any structure built on an ocean beach is temporary.

Just as the tides in coastal Virginia rise and fall twice each day, they also rise and fall on a much larger scale. Thousands of years ago, during the last Ice Age, when the polar caps held a large percentage of the earth's moisture, the beach was perhaps fifty miles east of where it is now. Thousands of years ago, the tide ebbed and turned, and now it is flood tide again. The beaches are heading westward.

In his lifetime, Lukei has seen the beach recede, the dunes migrate, the leeward myrtle thickets and marshes become

The myrtle thickets behind the dune line at Back Bay are a good place to spot yellow-rumped warblers and other birds.

filled with sand. Here at Back Bay, when viewed from one of the elevated dikes that make up freshwater impoundments at the refuge, the process is almost palpable. To the east is the ocean, and then comes the narrow berm of beach, the primary dune line reinforced by sand fencing, the myrtle and live oak thicket, the impoundments, the bayside marsh, and then to the west the brackish waters of the bay. On this low-slung finger of land, that panorama consumes less than a mile, often *much* less than a mile.

It is a fragile landscape, but one that is remarkable in its richness and diversity. In one view, we capture at least seven different habitats: ocean, beach, dunes, shrub thicket, salt marsh, freshwater marsh and ponds, and inland bay. Add to that the maritime forests of the highlands and the marshy islands of Back Bay, and the richness of the area is magnified even more.

Sea oats, along with American beach grass, is one of the most prolific dune plants on the southern Virginia coast.

Each habitat has its own constituency, and all exist together to form a typical barrier island ecosystem. Scoters and old-squaws gather in great rafts offshore. Striped bass forage beyond the surf. Ghost crabs burrow in the beach sand. Sea oats grow in the dunes. Warblers pick berries in myrtle thickets. Black ducks dabble on the freshwater ponds. Cottonmouth moccasins stalk bullfrogs in the marsh. Sunfish scour nesting sites in the shallow bay.

Other than the remote islands of the Eastern Shore, the Back Bay–False Cape area is the wildest,

Cottonmouth moccasins are numerous at Back Bay.

most unspoiled coastal ecosystem in Virginia. And the agencies that manage it intend to keep it that way.

Back Bay National Wildlife Refuge includes 8,000 acres, mainly salt and brackish marsh, and four miles of ocean beach. Neighboring False Cape State Park has 4,321 acres and six miles of beach. So together, this federal refuge and state park provide a natural area of vital importance to creatures as varied as loggerhead turtles, prothonotary warblers, and greater snow geese.

Back Bay National Wildlife Refuge

Like many of the wildlife refuges in the various North American flyways, Back Bay was created for the benefit of waterfowl, principally greater snow geese, whose numbers had fallen precipitously in 1938 when the Back Bay refuge was created by Presidential Proclamation. In 1939, waterfowl were given further protection when 4,600 acres of bay waters within the refuge boundaries were closed to hunting, also by Presidential Proclamation.

BACK BAY NATIONAL WILDLIFE REFUGE

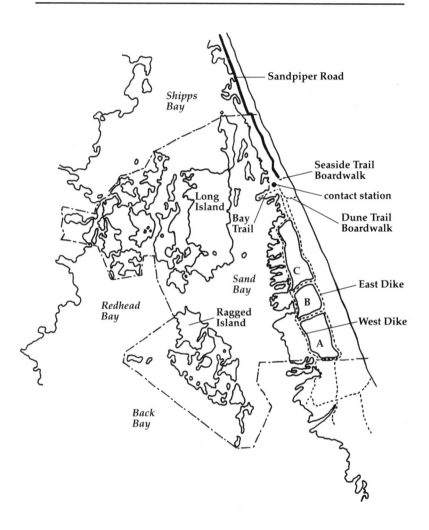

Sandpiper Road

Shipps
Bay

Seaside Trail
Boardwalk

contact station

Long
Island

Dune Trail
Boardwalk

Bay
Trail

C

East Dike

Sand
Bay

B

Redhead
Bay

Ragged
Island

West Dike

A

Back
Bay

Back Bay, of course, was known for the hunting of water-fowl long before it became a bastion of protection. The Princess Anne and Ragged Island hunting clubs were among those located on what is now the refuge site. The former was located near the parking area at the visitor center, and lumber from the large, three-story clubhouse was used to construct several of the original refuge buildings, including a boathouse. These hunting clubs, and others in the area, were founded in the latter part of the nineteenth century and attracted hundreds of wealthy sportsmen from northern cities as well as Tidewater. Local people worked as guides, cooks, and decoy makers, supplementing income that came largely from farming or seafood harvesting.

The Back Bay that you see today is not the same natural area visited by sportsmen in 1900. The mandate of the wildlife refuge was to benefit migrating waterfowl, and this has been achieved by the construction of various water control devices. It was during the 1950s and 1960s that refuge managers nation-wide began installing structures such as dams, dikes, and spillways. Back Bay got its first impoundments during those days, and they have been enlarged and improved in the intervening years.

Most of the hiking and biking trails at Back Bay run along the crests of dikes that contain the impoundments. Pumps and sluice gates are used to control the depth of the water. In the summer, the impoundments are emptied, and various seed-producing plants are allowed to grow. In fall, just prior to the arrival of the waterfowl, water is pumped from Back Bay into the impoundments, creating shallow ponds with depths from about one to four feet. The former are designed to benefit geese, dabbling ducks, and shorebirds, and the latter are favored by diving ducks such as scaup. So from fall through winter, the waters of Back Bay support a remarkable number of waterfowl, from the blue-winged teal that begin arriving in

Lesser scaup are diving ducks and can sometimes be spotted in the deeper impoundments at Back Bay.

September to the huge flocks of snow geese that will number in the thousands by February.

But that's not all. Although the refuge was built for waterfowl, its benefits extend far beyond birds with webbed feet, and management decisions are now made with a much broader constituency in mind. The myrtle thickets behind the primary dunes, for example, are important for migrating songbirds, as are the maritime forests of loblolly pine and live oak. The ocean beach is one of the northernmost nesting sites for endangered loggerhead turtles, and refuge officials recently began a program of transferring eggs to an enclosed area until they hatch, thus protecting them from predators such as gulls, fish crows, and raccoons. The shallow impoundments intended for ducks and geese are equally important to a variety of shorebirds, and water levels are maintained at optimum levels for them during their May migration to nesting sites.

The refuge is managed to benefit wildlife, and although some recreational use is allowed, the needs of the birds and turtles come first. In a highly populated area that gets millions of seasonal tourists, this is not always a popular course of action. For example, the beach is closed to swimming and sunbathing, although surf fishing and shell collecting are allowed. Motor vehicles are not allowed on the beach (with a few exceptions), nor on the roads atop the dikes. Motor vehicles and heavy beach use would damage nesting areas for loggerheads and various bird species, and traffic in the impoundment areas would disturb wintering waterfowl.

The refuge's policy of limiting vehicle traffic has sometimes created a prickly relationship with its neighbor to the south, False Cape State Park. The problem is, the only way to get to the park is through the wildlife refuge or to go by boat. So if the refuge limits access to its dike roads during winter, False Cape is virtually cut off, unless you want to take a ten-mile round-trip hike down the beach. Negotiations are currently under way to provide limited year-round public access.

When You Visit . . .

Take Sandpiper Road south from Sandbridge and you'll end up in the parking lot at the visitor center. As you drive into the refuge and pass the fee booth, the dunes and ocean are on your

Green-winged teal are early arrivals at Back Bay and False Cape each fall. Look for them in shallow ponds where there is grass and other plant growth.

left, a thicket of wax myrtle and bayberry on your right. The thicket is a good place to look for warblers during spring and fall migrations; yellow-rumped warblers are there through the winter.

The visitor center, though small, has an interesting collection of taxidermy mounts and artifacts, including decoys used during Back Bay's sporting club era. A canoe launch and fishing area are located adjacent to the parking lot, as are a series of foot trails and boardwalks, which in winter provide an excellent view of waterfowl on Back Bay.

The dike road begins just east of the visitor center and runs along the impoundments and through a maritime forest to False Cape State Park, a distance of 4.25 miles. From the visitor center to the North Carolina state line, it's nine miles. The dike road is open to hikers and bikers only, and portions of it may be closed seasonally to protect waterfowl. It would be a good idea to call the refuge before visiting to determine accessibility.

In most seasons, a hike or bike ride along the dikes is rewarding. In spring, resident waterfowl are pairing off and nesting, and the shallow impoundments get thousands of mi-

Snapping turtles are plentiful in the impoundments at Back Bay and False Cape. They have powerful jaws, so don't venture too close.

grating shorebirds. Neotropical songbirds are passing through, but most are found in the myrtle thickets and the forested area south of the impoundments. Wildflowers bloom in the marsh and along the dike road.

In summer, there are shorebirds foraging in the shallow water, killdeer and sandpipers on the exposed flats, and turtles basking in the sun. Ospreys begin nesting on their raised platforms in March and continue to feed their hatchlings through the summer. In late summer, look for marsh hibiscus blooming along the marsh edges.

Fall marks the arrival of migratory waterfowl, beginning in September with teal. It also marks the return trip of songbirds that nested north of the area to the southern United States and Central and South America for the winter. Fall is the time to go hawk watching; look for peregrine falcons and merlins along the beach and northern harriers patrolling the marshes.

During winter, large numbers of greater snow geese are on the refuge, along with Canada geese and other waterfowl. The best time to go is after a winter storm north of the area, which sends birds packing for more favorable climes. It is also a good time to look for pelagic birds. Sea ducks such as scoters and old-squaws can be seen on the ocean, along with cormorants, red-breasted mergansers, and northern gannets.

On your way to or from Back Bay, consider stopping at the Virginia Marine Science Museum, an excellent facility with a large aquarium and many other exhibits that feature the natural life of the Virginia coast. The museum is on General Booth Boulevard, just south of the Rudee Inlet bridge.

Wildness quotient: Six during summer, eight during winter. Back Bay gets surprisingly few visitors, considering the number of people who live within an hour's drive, and most who do come don't wander far from the visitor center and the nearby foot trails. So the wildness quotient rises in proportion to the amount of distance you put between yourself and the parking lot.

For information: Back Bay National Wildlife Refuge, 4005 Sandpiper Road, Virginia Beach, VA 23456. Phone (757) 721-2412.

False Cape State Park

False Cape State Park, on the Virginia Outer Banks, is accessible only by foot or by bicycle, making it one of the most remote public parks in the state. Access is by the dike roads through Back Bay National Wildlife Refuge or by beach. During some periods in winter, the dike roads may be closed to protect waterfowl, and at those times the only access is by beach or by boat.

Like Back Bay, False Cape includes many of the old hunting club properties, and several of the former club buildings are being used as staff residences and offices. One, the former Swan Club, is now an environmental education center, providing dormitory and meeting space for groups that come to study the barrier island ecosystem.

Over the years, some manipulation has taken place, but False Cape provides a near-wilderness experience. Canals were dug years ago to benefit the waterfowl, and trails have been established, but False Cape has a minimum of infrastructure.

Indeed, False Cape was a much busier community a century ago than it is today. Some three hundred people lived in the community of Wash Woods, named for the overwash that inundated the island during storms. There was a school, two churches, and many residences serving the farmers, fishermen,

FALSE CAPE STATE PARK

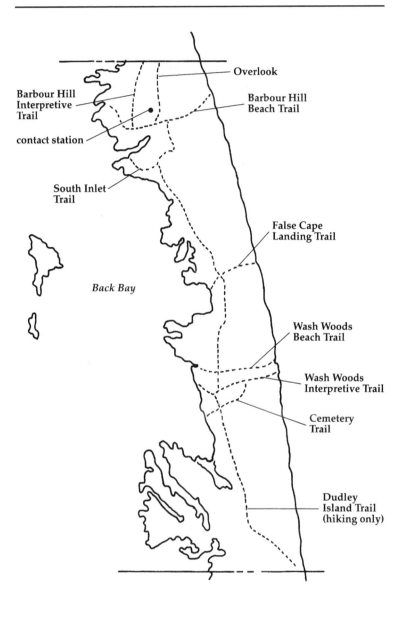

Overlook

Barbour Hill
Interpretive
Trail

Barbour Hill
Beach Trail

contact station

South Inlet
Trail

False Cape
Landing Trail

Back Bay

Wash Woods
Beach Trail

Wash Woods
Interpretive Trail

Cemetery
Trail

Dudley
Island Trail
(hiking only)

and hunting guides who made up the community. Little remains today. After experiencing too many overwashes and seeing the fertile farmland become covered with the sand of the westward-moving beach, Wash Woods residents also moved westward, to the mainland.

You can walk the trails of False Cape today and see evidence of the community. A short distance off a dune trail, in a shaded maritime forest, is the brick foundation of a church and the remains of a shingled steeple. Not far away is a cemetery where the Wash Woods families are buried—the Waterfields, the Palettes, and others—a few graves decorated by whelk shells.

When You Visit . . .

Call ahead to determine accessibility. In any case, be prepared for a walk or bike ride of at least twelve miles, in and out. The dike roads are made of well-packed sand and clay laced with gravel, so under most conditions the surface is good. If the dike roads are closed, you will have to walk on the beach. This is easier at low tide, when you can walk on the hard sand near the water's edge.

There are primitive camping areas and pit toilets, but not potable water, so bring your own. The Environmental Education Center is available for small groups, with shuttle service provided from Little Island Park near the entrance of Back Bay National Wildlife Refuge.

The best times to go are spring and fall, mainly for the migrating birds. The extensive maritime forest is heavily used by warblers and other migrants. May, September, and October are good months, especially after a weather front has moved through.

Wildness quotient: Eight

For information: False Cape State Park, 4001 Sandpiper Road, Virginia Beach, VA 23456. Phone (757) 426-7128.

8   FIRST LANDING STATE PARK

Summer tourists. Seafood restaurants. An active nightlife. Cruisers. Surfers. Bikinis. The Boardwalk. Bumper to bumper on Atlantic Avenue. The pervasive aroma of french fries and suntan oil. These are the general impressions of Virginia Beach, particularly among people who don't live there. Local residents and regular visitors have a few secrets, however, among them an oasis of cypress forest, Spanish moss, woodland trails, herons, warblers, and peace and quiet, even during those feverish days between Memorial Day and Labor Day.

First Landing State Park is that oasis, a great green wedge driven into the heart of one of the busiest vacation spots on the East Coast. First Landing begins at Shore Drive (Va. Route 60) about three miles east of the Chesapeake Bay Bridge-Tunnel. It extends along Shore Drive to Atlantic Avenue and ends at 64th Street, where there is a second access point. The main entrance and visitor center are near the western perimeter of the park off Shore Drive. First Landing was originally named Seashore State Park, but the name was changed in 1996 to commemorate the arrival at Cape Henry of the ship *Sarah Constant* and her captain, Christopher Newport of the London Company, who set ashore here on April 26, 1607, more than two weeks before finally settling at Jamestown.

At 2,770 acres, First Landing is a remarkable natural area, and not simply because it is an oasis of nature amid such a tide of vacationing humanity. As far as amateur naturalists are concerned, it would be worth regular visits no matter where it was located.

Let's begin with the cypress forest. There's a nice one just

FIRST LANDING STATE PARK

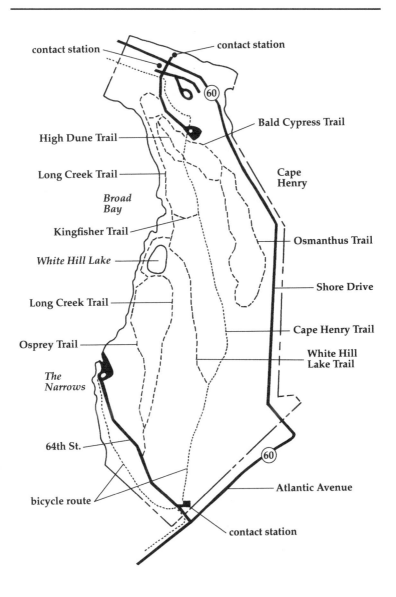

contact station

contact station

60

Bald Cypress Trail

High Dune Trail

Cape
Henry

Long Creek Trail

Broad
Bay

Kingfisher Trail

Osmanthus Trail

White Hill Lake

Shore Drive

Long Creek Trail

Cape Henry Trail

Osprey Trail

White Hill
Lake Trail

The
Narrows

64th St.

60

Atlantic Avenue

bicycle route

contact station

behind the visitor center and several patches elsewhere, notably along Cape Henry Trail, the bike route connecting the visitor center and 64th Street. What we have here is one of the northernmost stands of bald cypress in North America. Although there are larger cypress tracts on the Eastern Shore of Maryland, the one at First Landing is special because it is festooned with Spanish moss, giving the forest an emphatically southern, Faulkneresque quality.

Spanish moss is an epiphyte, meaning that it gets its nutrients from air and moisture, both of which it prefers on the warm side. That's why Spanish moss is plentiful in the southeastern coastal states but is on Virginia's endangered species list.

Bald Cypress Trail is a circuit of about a mile and a half that begins and ends at the visitor center. The park has an excellent guide to the trail that is available for a modest fee at the center. For those in a hurry or with physical limitations, the trail can be shortened by half by returning on the Cape Henry Trail, which bisects Bald Cypress. Maps are available free of charge.

The cypress forest at First Landing is near the northern limit of the range for the species. Like the trees found in southern swamps, those at the state park are festooned with Spanish moss.

Colorful prothonotary warblers, sometimes called swamp canaries, like freshwater wetlands. Look for them in the boggy areas near the visitor center at First Landing.

The character of the cypress forest changes with the seasons. In summer, the shallow ponds may be nearly dry, and wildlife may be at an ebb, but in spring, after a soaking rain, the soggy forest comes alive with birds and animals. First Landing is an important area for migrating songbirds, and cypress woods are especially good for birds that prefer a watery environment. Among the warblers, the prothonotary is an avid swamp-lover. It can be seen from spring to fall, as long as there is water to attract the insects it prefers to dine on. The swamps are also important to wading birds, most notably the green heron, which is seen regularly along the Bald Cypress Trail.

First Landing has more than seventeen miles of trails, some for hikers only, others for hikers and bicyclists. Bald Cypress is the most popular trail in the park, but if you want more distance and diversity (and fewer fellow travelers), try Osmanthus Trail, a 3.1-mile loop named after the *Osmanthus*, or wild olive tree. The trail is basically an extension of Bald Cypress, running easterly through wooded lowlands. It's a good place to see pileated woodpeckers and, in spring and fall, a variety of migrating songbirds. If you go during the warmer months, take along something to drink and insect repellent.

First Landing is not a wilderness setting. You can see a great variety of birds here and enjoy the sights and sounds of the cypress forest, but there are hundreds of thousands of people within a fairly small radius of the park, so don't expect to have the place to yourself.

Nature trails, built presumably to enable humans to watch wildlife, also have other purposes, not the least of which is an aerobic workout. Be prepared to see men in jogging shorts, women in sports gear, and purposeful young people of all ages pedaling their mountain bikes up and down dune trails. If you hear heavy breathing coming from the sassafras thicket up the trail, it is likely someone attempting a personal-best time from the visitor center to the boat ramp on Broad Bay.

I too enjoy a brisk bike ride down Cape Henry Trail, the trees all a blur, my metabolism sucking up that Big Mac, the wind whipping through what used to be my hair. If I feel the

The boardwalk and trail system at First Landing provides access to freshwater pools and their constituent wildlife species.

need to see birds, I stop and look around, fetch the binoculars from the fanny pack, and look for black-and-white warblers in the tops of the pines.

The designated bike route at First Landing is Cape Henry Trail, which you can pick up either at the contact station at 64th Street or at the visitor center. The trail extends the length of the park, crosses 64th Street, and then runs parallel to 64th along Broad Bay to The Narrows, where a boat ramp and concession stand are located. It's an out-and-back ride of about twelve miles.

Cape Henry is a trail for wide-tire all-terrain bikes. It's not a difficult run, but sandy patches, exposed tree roots, and the occasional muddy spots make it precarious for persnickety road bikes that prefer their pavement smooth and unblemished. The section of trail between the visitor center and 64th Street is smooth and well worn, a sand and clay surface tightly packed by traffic. It's just wide enough to allow two bikes to pass without undue alarm.

My favorite section is the shorter, narrower portion that goes from 64th Street to The Narrows. The trail follows a wooden bridge through a cypress woods and then enters an old dune area where it becomes somewhat hilly, at least by Tidewater standards. Soft sand in spots provides evidence of the geological history of the area, but it can also land you on your tush if you're not careful.

The trail crosses a swale where an emergency salt marsh has overtaken what once was a pine woods. The dead trees that remain in the marsh provide excellent nesting cavities for a variety of birds, ranging from crow-sized pileated woodpeckers to little brown-headed nuthatches. A wooden bridge with a lookout platform crosses the swale. It's a good spot to look for nesting ospreys from late March to October. A variety of hawks, principally northern harriers, can be seen over winter.

The trail parallels the shoreline of Broad Bay, now and then offering nice views of the water. It ends at the parking lot at The Narrows, where there is a small beach with the usual crabbers and fishermen and the ubiquitous personal watercraft.

When You Visit . . .

During the warmer months, go early in the morning and on weekdays. You'll avoid the heat and have the trails nearly to yourself. Bring insect repellent, since mosquitoes are

Green herons can be seen, and more often heard, in the wetland area of the state park.

part of nature's mix at First Landing. Ticks and chiggers will attack you if you venture off the trails into the underbrush.

If you ride a bike, ride it only on the bike trail. In the past, unthinking and discourteous people have damaged the dune environment because of off-road riding.

Cape Henry Trail, the bike route, is a good access route to hiking trails. For example, it intersects with High Dune Trail, Bald Cypress Trail (twice), Kingfisher Trail, and White Hill Lake Trail. Park and secure your bike and proceed on foot.

Early fall mornings are the best time to look for warblers

along Bald Cypress and Cape Henry Trails, especially just after a weather front has passed through the area. On winter days, look for hawks on the bridge on Cape Henry Trail and water-fowl on Broad Bay.

First Landing also offers primitive camping, cabins, a picnic area, and interpretive programs.

Wildness quotient: Four in the summer, but give it a seven in February. First Landing is a valuable natural area, and it probably looks today much as it did two hundred years ago when ships would anchor offshore and send parties ashore to get freshwater from the cypress swamp. Still, a park that gets thousands of visitors a year is not going to provide a wilderness experience.

For information: First Landing State Park, 2500 Shore Drive, Virginia Beach, VA 23451, or write Virginia State Parks, 203 Governor Street, Suite 306, Richmond, VA 23219. Phone number at the visitor center is (757) 481-4836.

9   CHESAPEAKE BAY
       BRIDGE-TUNNEL

What's this, you say? An outstanding natural area made of
concrete and steel and asphalt? Was that a tractor-trailer that
just rumbled by? Well, okay. Here we stand in an empty parking lot, and there are tractor-trailers going by, not to mention
cars, vans, pickup trucks, and the occasional motor home.
We're six miles out at sea. On our left is the Atlantic Ocean,
and on our right is Chesapeake Bay. It's the dead of winter. It's
cold out here. And there are birds all around.

The four rock islands that anchor the two tunnels of the
Chesapeake Bay Bridge-Tunnel are the best places in Virginia
to watch seabirds. In winter, after a hard freeze or two, the
islands are surrounded by thousands of scoters, old-squaws,
cormorants, and other diving ducks. If we get a lengthy freeze
that ices over the tidal creeks of the mainland, we might even
get some surface-feeding ducks out here.

The rock islands are highly regarded by fish, and fishermen,
because the nooks and crannies of the rock piles hold a great
store of small fish and mollusks. But by January, most of the

*All three North American
scoter species can be seen
on the bridge-tunnel.
The black scoter is a
regular winter
visitor.*

Winter is the best time to visit the bridge-tunnel because the number of sea ducks will be at its peak. Dress warmly and bring your binoculars and spotting scope.

fish and fishermen are gone, and the birds flock to the islands to dive for mussels and other shellfish that have attached themselves to the rocky bottom. These sea ducks are accomplished divers and can easily go down more than one hundred feet and remain submerged for minutes at a time.

Three of the four islands are normally closed to the public, but the good folks who run the bridge-tunnel complex have made a special concession to birders and other naturalists. Call or write to the Chesapeake Bay Bridge and Tunnel District (PO Box 111, Cape Charles, VA 23310-0111; phone [757] 331-2960) and ask for permission to observe birds and waterfowl from the four man-made islands. You will receive a letter of permission covering the calendar year, along with a brief list of instructions, most of which have to do with your safety.

When You Visit . . .

Show your letter of permission to the toll taker when you enter the facility, and the police will be informed of your intention to watch birds on the islands. Those without letters are allowed to stop on only one of the islands—the one where the snack bar, restrooms, fishing pier, and concomitant tourists are

located. Birding is good there, but it is better on the unpopu-
lated islands.

Take your binoculars, scope, and a good guide to seabirds
and waterfowl. Traveling from the north, you can island hop
at your leisure and end up on the southern island in time for
lunch at the Sea Gull Pier. For safety reasons, only right turns
are allowed, so begin with island one, head south to island
two, and so on.

Winter is the time to go—in January and February. Weather
conditions may be bitter, so dress warmly and be prepared to
see a multitude of waterbirds you won't find at most wildlife
refuges. Expect to see all three species of scoters, hundreds of
old-squaws, eiders, gulls, ruddy turnstones, purple sandpipers, buffleheads, ruddy ducks, redheads, canvasbacks, scaup,
and common goldeneye. There might even be a few dabblers;
we've seen black ducks and gadwalls on recent visits.

You will see basically the same mix of birds on all four
islands, but hit them all anyway. There might be a rare gull or
seabird hiding among the congregation. Look for snow bun-
tings along the grassy strips that line the tunnel walls. Ruddy
turnstones can be seen in the parking area, and purple sand-

*During the harshest
winter months, rafts of
hundreds of long-tailed
ducks gather along the
bridge to feed on shellfish.*

Northern gannets are large white birds with black wing-tips. They can be seen over the ocean waters, occasionally diving for fish.

pipers on the rocky shoreline. The rock jetties may have both double-crested and great cormorants. It is also worthwhile to stop at the parking lot at the north terminal and scan the fields and shrubs beyond the fence, especially during the weeks of migration.

At this writing, construction was under way on the new parallel bridge span, and not all the islands were available at all times. Call the bridge-tunnel office to determine accessibility before visiting.

Wildness quotient: What the heck. Let's give it a six. There may be tractor-trailers whizzing by, but the bridge-tunnel puts us in an ocean environment in the dead of winter, even if there's little chance of getting seasick.

For information: Chesapeake Bay Bridge and Tunnel District, PO Box 111, Cape Charles, VA 23310-0111. Phone (757) 331-2960.

10 FISHERMAN ISLAND AND EASTERN SHORE OF VIRGINIA NATIONAL WILDLIFE REFUGES

The sparsely populated tip of Virginia's Eastern Shore is an excellent place for a naturalist to explore. Here, the Atlantic Ocean meets the Chesapeake Bay at Cape Charles. During fall migration, great flocks of songbirds gather to put on fat reserves before making the seventeen-mile crossing between Cape Charles and Cape Henry.

There are trails to walk and creeks to explore. Across Route 13 at Kiptopeke State Park (see Chapter 11), you can watch ornithologists band birds and get a close-up view of those confusing fall warblers. The narrowing tip of the Eastern Shore peninsula makes it an ideal birding area, with thousands of birds concentrated in a relatively small area during the peaks of the migrations. Fortunately, much of the land here is pro-

Brown pelicans were once rare on the Virginia coast but since the 1980s have expanded their range northward. They regularly nest on Fisherman Island.

*Royal terns are
beach nesters that
raise their young
in large colonies.
Fisherman has
had a large colony
of royal terns in
recent years.*

tected by the state, the federal government, or The Nature
Conservancy.

The peninsula has Kiptopeke State Park on the bay side,
Eastern Shore of Virginia and Fisherman Island National Wildlife Refuges on the sea side, plus Nature Conservancy ownership of most of Smith, Myrtle, and Ship Shoal Islands. The
state owns Mockhorn Island, a marshy inner island that has
one of the largest clapper rail populations in the state.

The Eastern Shore of Virginia National Wildlife Refuge
(ESVNWR) complex includes a 725-acre mainland site as well
as most of Fisherman Island, a separate refuge administered
by the ESVNWR. In recent years, Fisherman Island has had
large breeding populations of little blue herons, great egrets,
black-crowned night herons, brown pelicans, and various gulls
and terns. A large colony of royal terns has also been using the
island, plus a few unusual species such as white ibises and yel-
low-crowned night herons.

When You Visit . . .

You pass through Fisherman Island when entering the bridge-tunnel from the north, but stopping is not allowed. To protect the area and its wildlife, access is limited to special events, such as tours sponsored by the refuge or conservation organizations. Birders are welcome, however, at the neighboring mainland refuge, which until 1984 was a military installation. During World War II, gun emplacements were installed to protect the bay entrance. The Air Force operated a radar station at the site during the years following the war.

A short hiking trail covers woodland, open fields, and salt marsh. You can climb a set of steps and stand atop a gun emplacement and have a great view of Smith Island, Fisherman Island, the bridge-tunnel, and the expansive marshes. This is a fine spot for observing hawks during the fall migration, and you can see plenty of warblers and resident birds in the thick understory. A scope gives you a good look at breeding birds that use the salt marshes in May and June.

A second platform provides a closer look at the marsh but doesn't have such a panoramic view. This platform is at the end of a trail and boardwalk and is handicapped accessible.

The tip of the Eastern Shore peninsula is a great place to watch birds during fall migration because they tend to stop there before crossing the Chesapeake Bay. When cold weather sends woodcock flying south, they are numerous on the refuge.

Migrating songbirds, such as this hooded warbler, can be found in the wooded areas of the refuge in spring and fall. The greatest variety of songbirds appears in May and September.

You can see songbirds along the trail and boardwalk, and the marshes should yield tricolored herons, great blues, great and snowy egrets, rails, and various gulls and terns. Watch for northern harriers patrolling the marsh during fall and winter, as well as passing skeins of black ducks.

On the southeast edge of the refuge is a narrow tidal creek, providing marsh access via small boat or canoe. Drive past the hiking trails and bunkers, turn right, and proceed a short distance to a cul-de-sac. Limited parking is available here, and a fairly primitive launch area provides access. The road that branches off the cul-de-sac is private property and leads to a commercial boat launch and docking area that is not part of the refuge.

The modest refuge put-in is a good launching spot for canoeing, for those who want to do a little salt marsh exploration. The tidal creek winds through the marsh and emerges on the west in the southern part of Magothy Bay, which separates the mainland from Smith Island. It's best to avoid open water in a small boat, so confine your explorations to the marsh, where the dominant plant is cordgrass, *Spartina alterniflora*.

The marsh on the southern portion of ESVNWR contains numerous herons, egrets, and rails, so the birding is usually very good. The best times to visit are fall and winter for water-fowl and hawk watching. September and October see the largest concentrations of warblers, with the greatest variety occuring early in the period. By late October and early November, yellow-rumped warblers, winter residents here, are ubiquitous in the myrtle thickets and forests. The freshwater pond at the visitor center is usually good for wading birds and dabbling ducks.

Wildness quotient: Six. Unlike Back Bay and Chincoteague, Eastern Shore and Fisherman Island get few visitors. Although the hiking trails are disappointingly short, on most days you will have the place to yourself.

It is hoped that in the future the refuge will open up more of this unique area to the public. Since the refuge was created, most of the money spent for improvements has gone to construction and expansion of a visitor center. Although the displays and audiovisual aids are impressive, what visitors really want is more access to the spectacular natural areas of the tip of the peninsula.

For information: Eastern Shore of Virginia National Wildlife Refuge, 5003 Hallett Circle, Cape Charles, VA 23310. Phone (757) 331-2760.

11   KIPTOPEKE STATE PARK

Kiptopeke is the only state park on Virginia's Eastern Shore, and it provides one of the few public beaches on the peninsula. For an area surrounded by water, there are very few opportunities to wade in the surf on public land. The town of Cape Charles has a municipal beach on the Chesapeake, and Chincoteague National Wildlife Refuge and Assateague Island National Seashore provide ocean access. Nearly everything in between is privately owned. The Nature Conservancy allows day use on most of its fourteen islands, but all are accessible only by boat, making them beyond the reach of casual visitors. The Commonwealth of Virginia also owns island and salt marsh tracts, but the access is likewise limited.

Kiptopeke, then, has a lot going for it, not the least of which is easy access. Birds? Got 'em. Seashells? Got 'em. Camping facilities? Got them too. You can even go fishing and crabbing from the pier where the ferries used to dock before the Chesapeake Bay Bridge-Tunnel opened for business in 1964.

Kiptopeke is the best place in Virginia to see fall warblers. True, you'll have to go to the Blue Ridge to get Canada warblers and other high-elevation species, but for pure numbers and the chance to see birds at close range, Kiptopeke is the place to go.

The Virginia Society of Ornithology (VSO), with the help of the Virginia Department of Game and Inland Fisheries, began a banding program here in 1962, concentrating on Neotropical migrant songbirds—the warblers, tanagers, thrushes, and other birds that nest in North America but spend their winters in the tropics. The migrating birds use the tip of the Eastern Shore peninsula as a staging area before crossing the Chesapeake, resting and restoring the depleted fat reserves that fuel their flight.

Over the years, the VSO banding program at Kiptopeke has added immeasurably to what we know about songbird migration in the eastern corridor of North America, and it has raised the public's consciousness about these colorful birds, many of which have suffered from habitat loss either on their wintering grounds in the rain forests of Central America or along migration corridors in this country. The banding center has fueled many an amateur naturalist's interest in warblers, and some of those who once visited the center as curious guests have returned as volunteers to join in the work. Guests are welcome at the center, which operates daily from early September through October.

A satellite operation is a fall hawk watch, which has been conducted at Kiptopeke since 1977. A raised observation platform was constructed in 1994, allowing visitors and volunteer counters an excellent venue. The average fall count of hawks, falcons, and vultures is more than thirteen thousand. Sharp-shinned and Cooper's hawks make up the majority of the birds listed, but peregrine falcons, bald eagles, and ospreys are noted fairly often. The observation platform at Kiptopeke may be the best location on the coast to see migrating peregrines. One day in late September, we watched more than sixty fly past.

A bird-banding center operates at Kiptopeke in September and October. Visitors are welcome.

The hawk observation platform at Kiptopeke is a good place to spot a rare peregrine falcon.

Of the four major hawk stations in Virginia, this is the only one where falcons, sharp-shinned hawks, Cooper's hawks, and northern harriers are noted in quantity. The station is operated by the VSO and the Hawk Migration Association of North America.

Because Kiptopeke is actually on the bay side of the Eastern Shore, that is, on the Chesapeake instead of the Atlantic, it is not technically part of the barrier island lagoon system we associate with the Virginia coast. It is included here for two reasons. One, located near the tip of the peninsula, it includes much of the flora and fauna of the seaside. Two, it is simply too good to pass up.

Red-tailed hawks are common winter residents of the Kiptopeke area.

The beach at Kiptopeke is a typical bay beach: a long

berm, a very gradual slope, and a shallow water environment invaded by thousands of pesky stinging nettles sometime around the July 4 holiday. There are some unique features, however. Take a look at those shells. Many of them, especially the numerous jingle shells, are common to the seaside and are rarely found farther north in the bay. Last year we made a lamp of jingle shells, filling an old jar with shells and then adding lamp hardware and a shade. Every time I switch it on I'm reminded of Kiptopeke.

Farther up the bay, the open water and the beaches are separated from the mainland by vast salt marshes and slightly elevated stands of pine and cedar called hammocks. Near the Virginia-Maryland state line, near the town of Saxis, the marshes are miles wide. But here at Kiptopeke we have something altogether different. The bay breaks upon the shore, and just beyond the berm is a high primary dune, and behind it a secondary dune. It's a system very similar to that of the barrier islands.

When You Visit . . .

The trails at Kiptopeke should be hiked deliberately, with binoculars, field guides, and an inquiring mind. Fall and winter are the best times to go because the biting insects are gone, the winter birds are in, and the open woods give you an idea as to the form and function of a maritime forest.

September and October are ideal for the songbird migration. Visit the banding station and hone your identification skills, then take to the trails and put them to use. Midwinter is also one of my favorite times to visit. The shallow waters off the fishing pier usually have abundant diving ducks and sea ducks, and the myrtle thickets behind the dunes are filled with yellow-rumped warblers. I often combine a visit to Kiptopeke with a birding trip on the Chesapeake Bay Bridge-Tunnel. They are just a few miles apart.

The hiking trails and boardwalks at Kiptopeke give visitors a close look at the dunes and maritime forest.

At Kiptopeke, take the hiking trail on the south side of the roadway, beginning at the parking area across the road from the bathing beach. The trail—a boardwalk, actually—traverses a thicket of cedar and myrtle and runs along the ridge line of the dunes. Turn right and you begin a descent of one of the tallest maritime dunes on the Eastern Shore. Notice the vegetation, the plants and trees that grow along the ridge line at the higher elevations, away from the salt water. Notice how the plant communities change as the dune slopes toward the bay and finally flattens out to become a shrub community.

The breakwater of concrete ships just beyond the old ferry terminal is responsible for maintaining the shrub thicket and maritime dune. Stand on the walkway, look north and south, and you can see that the bay has covered what was once a shrub thicket and has eaten away the high dunes. White sandy scars are visible for several miles in each direction.

The forests and shrub thickets that remain at Kiptopeke are home to raccoons, gray squirrels, foxes, opossums, and other

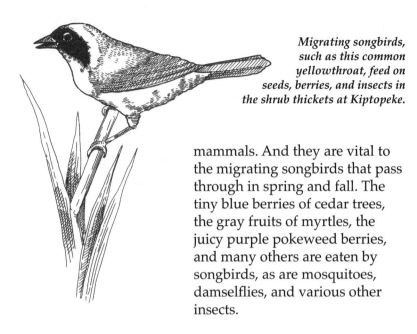

Migrating songbirds, such as this common yellowthroat, feed on seeds, berries, and insects in the shrub thickets at Kiptopeke.

mammals. And they are vital to the migrating songbirds that pass through in spring and fall. The tiny blue berries of cedar trees, the gray fruits of myrtles, the juicy purple pokeweed berries, and many others are eaten by songbirds, as are mosquitoes, damselflies, and various other insects.

The forest and shrub thicket are important, too, for other reasons. Birds are vulnerable to predators and foul weather when they travel in the open. They can be attacked by sharp-shinned hawks, and winds can blow them off course and out to sea. So the forest and shrub community provides cover, protection, and a place to rest, as well as food.

Various studies, including the results of banding surveys, indicate that a forested corridor along a migration route is vital. The Virginia coast, with a few exceptions, is still rural and largely wooded. Future community planning efforts should take into account the importance of a forested corridor for wildlife.

Wildness quotient: Six. The trails are interesting but short.

For information: Kiptopeke State Park, 3540 Kiptopeke Drive, Cape Charles, VA 23310. Phone (757) 331-2267.

12   THE NATURE CONSERVANCY'S VIRGINIA COAST RESERVE

This is the last of the coastal wilderness in the east—a fifty-thousand-acre preserve of beaches, bays, salt marsh, and upland. It is one of the few places left in America where you can spend a day walking a beach, exploring a marsh, or paddling a canoe without seeing another soul. When we think of wilderness, we envision mountain ranges in the West or in Alaska, but these remote islands that lie off Virginia's Eastern Shore are no less wild and no less special.

Along the unglaciated coast, from Long Island to Florida, no other barrier island ecosystem remains today much as it was when the European settlers found it in the seventeenth century. From the Virginia Capes and the entrance to Chesapeake Bay northward for some seventy-five miles, the islands, bays, and marshes bear precious little evidence of the human hand. There are no roads, parking lots, or visitor centers, only the occasional fisherman's shack and a handful of abandoned Coast Guard stations.

It nearly wasn't so. In the late 1960s, a group of New York investors purchased the three southernmost islands and announced plans for a lavish resort development, complete with golf course, hotels, condominiums, restaurants, and shops. There was talk that a bridge and causeway would link the resort to the mainland. But before ground could be broken, the project began to hit snags. Wetlands regulations, public opposition, and an economic recession dampened the developers' enthusiasm, and The Nature Conservancy made an offer for the islands. An agreement was reached, and thus began one

MARYLAND

VIRGINIA

Tangier
Island

*Pocomke
Sound*

Chincoteague

Assateague
Island

Wallops Island

Assawoman Island

Accomac

*Chesapeake
Bay*

Metomkin Island

Wachapreague

⑬

Cedar Island

Nassawadox

Parramore Island

Virginia
Coast Reserve
Headquarters

Hog Island

*Atlantic
Ocean*

N

Oyster

Cobb Island

Wreck Island

Ship Shoal Island

Myrtle Island

Smith Island

Fisherman Island

Chesapeake Bay
Bridge-Tunnel

VIRGINIA
COAST
RESERVE

The Nature Conservancy owns all or part of fourteen islands on the Virginia coast, comprising the Virginia Coast Reserve, a sanctuary of some 45,000 acres. Conservancy ownership includes Metomkin, Parramore, Hog, Cobb, Ship Shoal, Myrtle, and Smith Islands, as shown on the map, plus other smaller inland islands not shown.

of the largest and most important private land preservation projects in America.

At that time, The Nature Conservancy was a small conservation organization based in Arlington, Virginia. Its goal was to identify ecologically significant natural areas around the country and to protect them, usually through outright purchase. With the financial aid of the Mary Flagler Cary Charitable Trust and others, the Conservancy gradually increased its holdings over the years, forming the Virginia Coast Reserve, a sanctuary that today includes beaches, marshes, and adjacent seaside farmland.

The importance of the Virginia Coast Reserve was highlighted when the United Nations designated it an international biosphere reserve, citing it as a model of how humans should live in harmony with nature. The Nature Conservancy named the reserve one of the ten Last Great Places in America.

Like most wilderness areas, the barrier islands off the Eastern Shore are remote. Only two are accessible by bridge: Assateague, which is covered in Chapter 13, and neighboring Wallops, home of a NASA launch site and off-limits to the public. From Wallops south to Fisherman Island, a distance of some seventy-five miles, the islands are close to being in their natural state. Only Cedar Island, a portion of which was subdivided several years ago, remains largely in private hands. The remainder of the islands and marshes are protected by the federal or state government or by The Nature Conservancy, which is by far the largest landowner. The Virginia Coast Reserve includes all or part of fourteen islands.

The Conservancy allows day use on most of the islands in its sanctuary. Hiking, swimming, beachcombing, birdwatching, picnicking, and related activities are allowed. Overnight camping, motor vehicles, and pets are not allowed. There are no facilities on the islands.

When You Visit . . .

The easiest way to visit the Virginia Coast Reserve is to sign up for one of the field trips sponsored by the Conservancy. There are a dozen or so each year, mainly during the spring and fall months to coincide with the peaks of bird migration. Boat transportation is provided, and a staff naturalist leads the trip. It's the quickest way to learn about the island ecosystem, and if you don't have a boat, it's the only way to get there.

If you do have a boat, the Virginia Department of Game and Inland Fisheries operates numerous launch sites on the seaside. The major ones are at Chincoteague, Folly Creek, Wachapreague, Quinby, Willis Wharf, and Oyster. If you go by boat, be sure to have navigational charts, the required safety equipment, and food and drink.

The bays that separate the islands from the mainland are shallow, and navigation can be difficult. It's a good idea to get directions from knowledgeable local people before setting out. In general, the northern islands are easier to get to than the southern ones, because they are closer to the mainland and can be reached by marsh channels rather than by crossing wide bays. Folly Creek, for example, winds through the marsh and empties into the ocean at an inlet between Metomkin and Cedar Islands. Hog Island, in contrast, is separated from the mainland by Hog Island Bay, a ten-mile-wide, shallow estuary that can be very hazardous when the wind is blowing.

The barrier island lagoon system can also be explored from its mainland component at several locations. The Conservancy maintains a hiking trail across fields, woodlands, and salt marsh hammocks to Hog Island Bay. The trail is at Brownsville Farm, the Conservancy headquarters near Nassawadox. Public boat launching facilities on the seaside usually provide good birding venues or access to the mainland marshes.

Exploring Folly Creek

There are dozens of creeks and bays on the seaside Eastern Shore and not enough space to describe them all, so I've picked Folly Creek as a representative waterway. Access is by the state boat launching facility near Accomac at the end of county Route 651. I enjoy two types of trips on Folly Creek. One is by canoe, paddling from the boat launch westward to the head of the creek. The other is by motorboat, running out the creek to Cedar and Metomkin Islands and Burton's Bay.

Let's go canoeing first. Folly Creek is strongly tidal, with a rise and fall of as much as six feet per tidal cycle. It is a narrow creek, so the velocity of the current is high. For that reason, I plan my trips to the headwaters during the waning hour or so of flood tide. That way, I'll be paddling with the current to the head of the creek, and I'll be traveling with the ebbing tide when I return.

Exploring Folly by canoe is a leisurely day trip, but half a day will do if you're pressed for time. Folly is something of a blue-collar creek. People work on it, fishing for crabs and gathering oysters and clams, and recreational anglers like to go flounder fishing here. There are a few houses along the banks, some boat docks, but no fancy developments.

Once you put a little distance between your canoe and the boat dock, the creek takes on a wilder flavor. Folly splits into two branches as it nears an old plantation home called The Folly, and from here both branches become very shallow. Eagles have nested in recent years in tall pines along the right branch, and in winter, hundreds of green-winged teal and black ducks gather at a freshet at the head of the creek.

This is a wonderful place to explore, because the creek is too shallow for motorboats, and there is no development on the shoreline. The Nature Conservancy, in fact, owns the farm on

Orchard orioles
are frequent summer
visitors to woodlands and
farm fields of the Folly Creek area.

the north side of the creek. It's a great place to see birds, especially waterfowl in fall and winter and shorebirds during the migrations. Wading birds such as herons and egrets abound, and if you paddle all the way to the head of the creek and sit quietly beside a myrtle thicket, you should see a variety of warblers and other woodland birds.

Folly was once a fairly deep, navigable creek all the way to its headwaters. On the left bank, as you head up the creek, you can see the remains of an old oyster shucking house where seafood was packed and shipped to market during the early 1900s. The creek has silted in so badly, however, that the area is now accessible only by canoe. Here and there in the shallow water are little tumps of cordgrass that were not there a few years ago, an indication that the shallow creek may soon become a salt marsh.

For my motorboat trip, I have a sixteen-foot Chincoteague scow, which I find perfect for exploring the waters of Folly Creek and other seaside waterways. It draws little water and maneuvers easily through the twisting channels. Any similar small craft will get you out Folly Creek safely.

From the boat launch, the creek winds through a beautiful salt marsh, intersects the Intracoastal Waterway, and empties into an inlet between Cedar and Metomkin Islands. The channels and inlet are good places to catch flounder, and the tidal flats are good for clamming.

The inlet and the beaches surrounding it change on an almost daily basis. A few years ago, the inlet was about a quarter mile south of where it is at this writing. The inlet grew narrower and shallower and eventually closed, and a new one opened farther north, just south of Metomkin Island. You can't depend on nautical charts to navigate this area, so unlock the tilt lever on your outboard and be prepared to run aground.

If you go on the beach, be especially careful during early summer. Colonies of skimmers and terns and endangered piping plovers nest on the islands, principally on the flat overwash areas. They scrape shallow nests in the sand amid a scattering of shells, which offers perfect camouflage. Human disturbance greatly hampers the nesting success of these birds, so keep your distance. Most of the bird colonies are marked by signs posted by either the state or the Conservancy. The birds, too, will let you know when you venture too near.

The most visible landmark in the area is the abandoned U.S. Coast Guard station on the north end of Cedar Island. In this flat topography, the old station stands out like a gray ghost, looming over the marsh and beach. It was decommissioned in the early 1960s and is now privately owned.

The Intracoastal Waterway, a narrow, shallow "inside passage," runs the length of the Eastern Shore, allowing boaters to travel the seaside without having to enter the ocean through dangerous inlets. It intersects Folly Creek at two locations. A left turn going out the creek at green daymarker 87 takes you northward across Metomkin Bay to Gargatha and Kegotank

Terns, skimmers, and other birds nest in large colonies on the beaches of the Virginia Coast Reserve. If you visit the islands during nesting seasons, keep well away from the bird colonies.

Bays, which lie behind Metomkin and Assawoman Islands. Right turns at daymarkers 91 and 92 take you down Longboat Channel and across Burton's Bay to Wachapreague and points south. The waterway is subject to filling and is difficult to navigate in many places.

A Different Approach

Visiting these undeveloped and remote barrier islands is not for everyone. Unless you're experienced at handling a boat, you'd be better off going on one of the Conservancy tours or doing your marsh and beach exploration at more accessible sites, such as Assateague National Seashore or Chincoteague National Wildlife Refuge.

It takes a special mental approach to enjoy remote places such as these seaside marshes and islands. This is nature in the raw, and there are no interpretive guides, no nature trails, no park rangers. If you beach your boat on an ebbing tide, you're probably going to have to stay there until the tide turns. If you get hungry or thirsty, you're going to have to depend on what you brought with you.

These conditions energize some of us and intimidate others. For some, the crowds and interpretive trails at parks and refuges are off-putting, cheapening the experience of nature. For others, they provide a quick education, an insulating blanket of safety, an opportunity to share an experience.

One's comfort zone regarding nature in the raw hinges on two factors: an innate capacity for adventure, and actual experience with a particular place. I don't have a high capacity for adventure, but I have spent thousands of hours in a coastal setting and feel comfortable with it. I would rather spend my Saturday canoeing Folly Creek alone than hiking with a group tour at Assateague. Conversely, on my infrequent trips to the mountains, I feel most comfortable hiking well-marked trails, and if I have a guidebook or a park ranger to follow, so much the better.

The key, I suppose, is to know your own needs and limits. If you are new to these coastal ecosystems, it would be best to build your knowledge reserve and comfort zone by first going on guided excursions. Gradually, you can make the break to more independent exploration.

Wildness quotient: Ten. When it comes to a barrier island–salt marsh setting, this is as natural as it gets. There are parks and refuges all along the coast, but the Virginia Coast Reserve is large enough, and remote enough, to be special.

For information: Contact the Virginia Coast Reserve for information on tours, membership, and volunteer projects. The address is PO Box 158, Brownsville Farm, Nassawadox, VA 23413. Phone (757) 442-3049.

13 CHINCOTEAGUE NATIONAL WILDLIFE REFUGE AND ASSATEAGUE NATIONAL SEASHORE

Chincoteague National Wildlife Refuge, created in 1943, is one of numerous sanctuaries along the Atlantic flyway whose major constituency is migrating waterfowl. The brackish ponds, which were constructed in the early 1960s, are a magnet to snow geese, Canada geese, and a wide variety of dabbling ducks, as well as shorebirds.

Chincoteague National Wildlife Refuge is located on Assateague Island, the largest barrier island on the Virginia coast. The refuge is on the southern end of the island and is reached by taking Route 175 to the island town of Chincoteague and then crossing a bridge to the refuge. Since the bridge to Assateague opened in the 1960s, the refuge and the town have become tourist attractions, with more than a million visitors each year. Most come in the summer to go to the beach.

Assateague Island is thirty-seven miles long and is shared by Virginia and Maryland. Most of the Maryland portion is managed by the National Park Service as Assateague National Seashore. Most of the Virginia portion is in the refuge and is managed by the U.S. Fish and Wildlife Service. The state of Maryland operates a park on the extreme northern end of the island. Although this is a guide to the *Virginia* coast, it makes little sense to ignore half of an island simply because of a political boundary, so this chapter covers both the Chincoteague refuge in Virginia and Assateague National Seashore and State Park in Maryland.

During winter, snow geese gather on the impoundments at Chincoteague NWR by the thousands.

Chincoteague National Wildlife Refuge

Chincoteague is of interest to naturalists for a number of reasons. First, there are birds—lots of birds. Wintering waterfowl are a given, but the maritime forest on the southern portion of the island is a vital feeding and resting area for Neotropical migrants, those colorful warblers, tanagers, and related birds that nest in North America and winter in the tropics.

The shallow ponds and salt marshes that surround the island are home to herons, egrets, bitterns, rails, and other marsh birds. The tidal flats and ponds hold thousands of shorebirds during the peak of migration, and endangered piping plovers nest on the wide beach at the southern end of the island called The Hook.

Birding is good at Chincoteague nearly year-round. Waterfowl begin congregating in October and, depending on the weather, are on the refuge until spring. April and May are good months to see the Neotropical migrants, and the peak shorebird months are July and August. September and October mark the busiest days of the fall songbird and hawk migration,

CHINCOTEAGUE NATIONAL
WILDLIFE REFUGE

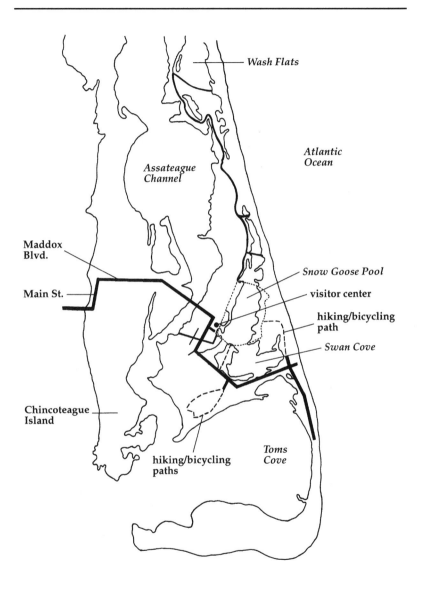

Wash Flats

Atlantic
Ocean

Assateague
Channel

Maddox
Blvd.

Main St.

Snow Goose Pool

visitor center

hiking/bicycling
path

Swan Cove

Chincoteague
Island

hiking/bicycling
paths

Toms
Cove

The hiking trails at Chincoteague NWR provide access to a maritime forest where many bird species can be seen, as well as endangered Delmarva fox squirrels.

with some warblers, notably the yellow-rumped, remaining on the refuge through the winter. There are also a large number of resident birds, bringing the total varieties that might be seen to more than three hundred.

Beyond birds, Chincoteague offers a beautiful beach, hiking trails through a maritime forest, many acres of salt marsh, and enough space so that you can escape the tourists and get some solitude. So if your interest is barrier island geology, salt marsh life, shell collecting, or birding, you can find many ways to spend your time at Chincoteague.

When You Visit . . .

Drive onto the island and pass the toolboth; a visitor center is on your left. A small interpretive display and a video production are available for viewing, and there are restrooms and a parking area. The Wildlife Loop, a paved 3.1-mile circuit, begins here. The loop is open to motor vehicles from 3 p.m. until dusk; the rest of the time, access is limited to hikers and bicyclists.

Other trails intersect Wildlife Loop, adding to the miles you can cover as well as the diversity of habitat. The loop runs along the earthen dikes that make up the brackish impoundments and then winds through a pine woods and wooded swamp. Black Duck Trail joins the southern portion of the loop and provides access for hikers and bicyclists to a second paved loop called Woodland Trail, a circuit of about a mile and a half. Another trail intersects Wildlife Loop, crosses a marsh, and runs behind the dune line to the northernmost parking lot at the beach.

Another option, available only to hikers, is the unpaved service road that branches off the loop and goes all the way to the Maryland line. A spur breaks off from the service road about two miles north of the visitor center and provides beach access for those who prefer to avoid the crowds.

If you want to see a barrier island beach in its natural state, you must go north. The dunes at the beach parking areas are sculpted by bulldozers rather than the forces of nature, because storm overwash would damage the brackish impoundments built for the waterfowl at Chincoteague. The bulldozed dune line extends some two miles up the beach like the Great Wall of China and then gives way to a beautiful natural landscape of rolling dunes and myrtle thickets. Most of the

The lighthouse on Assateague Island aided mariners for more than a century.

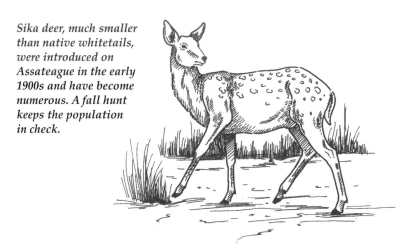

Sika deer, much smaller than native whitetails, were introduced on Assateague in the early 1900s and have become numerous. A fall hunt keeps the population in check.

dune area is off-limits, however, so you must view it from afar, or go to the Maryland end of the island.

There are no camping facilities on the Virginia portion of the island, but there are plenty on neighboring Chincoteague Island and on the mainland. There is also a wide range of hotels, motels, and restaurants. Bring binoculars for close viewing of birds. Spotting scopes are good for scanning the impoundments for shorebirds and waterfowl. Insect repellent is recommended during the warmer months.

In addition to birds, Chincoteague is also home to popular nonnative mammal species. The Chincoteague ponies have been on the island for decades, perhaps centuries. Sika deer, actually small Oriental elk, were introduced on the Maryland portion in the early 1900s and have flourished, making an annual hunt necessary to keep the population in check.

Whereas excess sikas are shot, excess ponies are sold. The ponies are the property of the Chincoteague Volunteer Fire Department, and each July they are rounded up by local "saltwater cowboys." On the third Wednesday of July, the ponies swim the channel between Assateague and Chincoteague and are herded down Main Street to the Carnival Grounds. The

The famous Chincoteague ponies are rounded up each July, and after making the swim from Assateague to Chincoteague, several dozen are sold at auction to benefit the local fire department.

next day, several dozen are sold at auction. The sale keeps the population in check and helps buy equipment for the fire department.

Theories abound as to how and when the ponies arrived on Assateague. Legend has it that they were aboard a Spanish galleon that wrecked off the island in the seventeenth century. A more likely, if less romantic, theory is that the ponies were among the animals pastured on the island by local landowners in the seventeenth and eighteenth centuries or later.

The wild ponies can be dangerous—they can bite and kick—so keep your distance. They can also cause tourists to do dumb things, like slamming on the brakes to get a better look.

Wildness quotient: In July near the beach parking areas, a two. Hike the service road to the wild beach, and the number rises to seven. In winter, the numbers are six and eight, respectively.

For information: Chincoteague National Wildlife Refuge, PO Box 62, Chincoteague, VA 23336. Phone (757) 336-6122.

Assateague National Seashore

The northern end of Assateague Island is much narrower than the southern end, with very little beach and a shrub thicket separating the ocean from Sinepuxent Bay. From atop the Verrazano Bridge on Route 611, you can get a panoramic view of a barrier island lagoon system. On your left is the resort community of Ocean City, which is separated from Assateague by Ocean City Inlet. The bridge crosses a shallow bay, and from it you can see the dune thickets, the beach, the salt marsh, and, to the south, the wider portion of the island where some maritime forest remains.

There are two highway accesses to the Maryland portion of Assateague: from the town of Berlin on Route 113, or from Ocean City on Route 611. In Berlin, turn east from Route 113 to Route 376 and go four miles to Route 611. Turn right and go five more miles to the Verrazano Bridge and Assateague. From Ocean City, take Route 611 from its intersection with Route 50 on the mainland just west of the island. It's a distance of about eight miles.

When You Visit . . .

The best way to explore this part of Assateague is by bicycle and by foot. A paved bike path begins at the parking area at the state park and extends southward parallel to Bayberry Drive some four miles to the cul-de-sac, where the pavement ends.

My favorite Assateague outing, especially during spring and fall, is to park the car at the state park, hop on my bike, and take a leisurely ride to the end of the road. Along the way there are trails to explore, myrtle thickets to investigate, and an ocean to splash around in should I feel the need to cool off.

CHINCOTEAGUE NATIONAL WILDLIFE REFUGE AND ASSATEAGUE NATIONAL SEASHORE

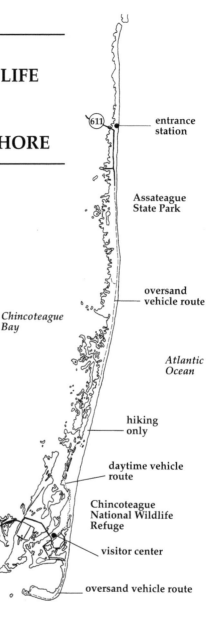

611

entrance
station

Assateague
State Park

oversand
vehicle route

*Chincoteague
Bay*

*Atlantic
Ocean*

hiking
only

daytime vehicle
route

Chincoteague
National Wildlife
Refuge

175

visitor center

oversand vehicle route

The bike trail from the state park to the national seashore entrance is straight and fairly dull, but it runs along a dense wooded thicket where warblers can be seen during spring and fall migrations. These duneland shrub thickets, consisting mainly of bayberry and closely related wax myrtle, attract thousands of yellow-rumped warblers each winter. The birds feed on the blue-gray berries of the myricas and, through their droppings, help extend the margins of the shrubland.

The national seashore entrance station is about two miles from the state park parking lot. Just beyond the station, on the right, is one of three side trails worth exploring. Bayside Drive extends less than a mile to a parking area on Sinepuxent Bay, where canoe and bike rentals are available. Along the drive are numerous camping areas, and the combination of cleared grasslands and shrub thickets creates edge habitat where many birds can be seen. I call this area Catbird Point because there are more gray catbirds residing here than any place I know of on the coast. This little finger of land is also an inviting stop for various migrant songbirds, and unusual sightings are made fairly often during the migrations.

Assateague offers three nature trails (for hikers only), and the first begins here on Bayside Drive. The Life of the Marsh Trail is a loop that extends over and through a salt marsh setting on the edge of the bay. This is a good trail for studying marsh plants. You'll see everything from salt marsh cordgrass (*Spartina alterniflora*) and salt meadow hay (*Spartina patens*), which are associated with a high-saline environment, to plants of the transition zone and brackish water.

The tidal zone at the water's edge is the place to find cordgrass. In slightly higher areas, where water covers the plants only during extreme high tides, you can see salt meadow hay lying in thick cowlicks. Mixed in is salt grass (*Distichlis spicata*) and black needlerush (*Juncus roemerianus*). In the higher marsh look for *Salicornia*, a tubular plant that usually grows in colonies. Sea lavender (*Limonium carolinianum*) and sea oxeye (*Borrichia frutescens*) also grow there. The former has tiny lavender flowers from July to October, and the latter has bright yellow blossoms in summer and prickly brown seed heads in fall and winter.

As the elevation rises slightly, look for shrubs such as marsh elder (*Iva frutescens*), groundsel (*Baccharis halimifolia*), wax myrtle (*Myrica cerifera*), and bayberry (*Myrica pensylvanica*). Loblolly pine and wild black cherry dominate the upper elevations, along with vines such as poison ivy and greenbrier. In winter, this is a good trail to view waterfowl feeding in the shallow waters of Sinepuxent Bay.

The two other trails are the Life of the Forest Trail and the Life of the Dunes Trail, both loops of about half a mile. The forest trail is especially good for seeing migrating songbirds and resident birds that prefer a forested environment, such as the rufous-sided towhee. Take your binoculars, a bird guide, and insect repellent. If the weather is warm, mosquitoes will be abundant.

The dune trail provides a fascinating look at how sand dunes form and how they are sculpted by wind, water, and other forces. The dune environment changes rapidly, so after several visits over a period of time, it is possible to document such changes and speculate on how and why they happened. The trail also provides a close-up look at some of the most fascinating plants of the coast, species such as American beach grass, beach heather, seaside goldenrod, purple gerardia, blue toadflax, and seabeach evening primrose. These plants, with their extensive root systems, play an important role in stabilizing the dunes, and many of them brighten the landscape with beautiful flowers.

Canada geese are year-round residents; the population rises in winter with the arrival of migratory birds from the north.

When you go to Assateague, don't miss the visitor station on the mainland just west of the bridge. It has excellent exhibits, including a large aquarium, bookshop, and other features.

Bring sunscreen if you plan to spend much time on the beach. The state park has a concession at the bathhouse that sells sandwiches and snacks.

Campsites are available behind the primary dunes, and farther up-island along Bayside Drive. Walk-in campsites are at the north end of the paved road and will appeal to those who are willing to swap some creature comforts for privacy.

Wildness quotient: As on the Virginia end, it increases in proportion to how much distance you put between yourself and the crowds and "improvements." In fact, I give it the same numbers: In July near the beach parking areas, a two. Hike southward down the beach, and the number rises to seven. In winter, the numbers are six and eight, respectively.

Bridge to Assateague, Maryland

For information: Assateague Island State Park, 7307 Stephen Decatur Highway, Berlin, MD 21811-9741. Phone (410) 641-2120. Assateague Island National Seashore, Route 611, 7206 National Seashore Lane, Berlin, MD 21811. Phone (410) 641-3030.